Uxbridge Ontario Book 1 in Colour Photos, Saving Our History One Photo at a Time

Photography
by Barbara Raué
©2022

Series Name: Cruising Ontario

Book 218: Uxbridge Book 1

Cover photo: 127 Brock Street East, Page 37

©All the photos in this book have been taken with my cameras. I own the rights to them.

Series Name: Cruising Ontario
Saving Our History One Photo at a Time
in colour photos

Books Available in Alphabetical Order:
Aberfoyle, Acton, Ajax, Alton, Amherstburg, Ancaster, Arthur, Auburn, Aylmer, Ayr, Beaver Valley, Belgrave, Belleville, Bloomingdale, Blyth, Brantford, Brockville, Burford, Burlington, Caledon, Caledonia, Cambridge, Carlow, Chatsworth, Clifford, Collingwood, Conestogo, Delhi, Dorchester to Aylmer, Drayton, Drumbo, Dundas, Dunlop, Eden Mills, Elmira, Elora, Erin, Essex, Fergus, Goderich, Grimsby, Guelph, Hagersville, Hamilton, Hanover, Harriston, Hespeler, Jarvis, Kingston, Kingsville, Kitchener, Lake Superior, Lincoln, Linwood, Listowel, London, Lucknow, Merrickville, Mono, Mount Forest, Mount Pleasant, Neustadt, New Hamburg, Newboro, Newport, Niagara-on-the-Lake, Niagara Falls, North Bay, Oakville, Onondaga, Orangeville, Orillia, Oshawa, Owen Sound, Palmerston, Paris, Pelham, Perth, Peterborough, Petrolia, Pickering, Port Colborne, Port Elgin, Portland, Preston, Rockwood, Sarnia, Sault Ste. Marie, Seaforth, Sheffield, Shelburne, Simcoe, Smiths Falls, Smithville, Southampton, St. Catharines, St. George, St. Jacobs, St. Marys, St. Thomas, Stoney Creek, Stratford, Thamesford, Thunder Bay, Tillsonburg, Toronto, Waterdown, Waterford, Waterloo, Welland, Wellesley, West Flamborough, Westport, Whitby, Windsor, Wingham, Woodstock

Book 201-202: Whitby
Book 203: Ajax, Pickering
Book 204-206: Oshawa
Book 207-209: Niagara Falls
Book 210: North Bay
Book 211: Fort Erie

Book 212-215 Haldimand County
Book 216: Sudbury
Book 217: Parry Sound
Book 218-219: Uxbridge

Table of Contents

Brock Street West	Page 5
Brock Street East	Page 22
Railway Street	Page 39
Young Street	Page 41
Dominion Street	Page 42
First Avenue	Page 48
Second Avenue	Page 54
Toronto Street South	Page 56
Colborne Street	Page 69
Peel Street	Page 69

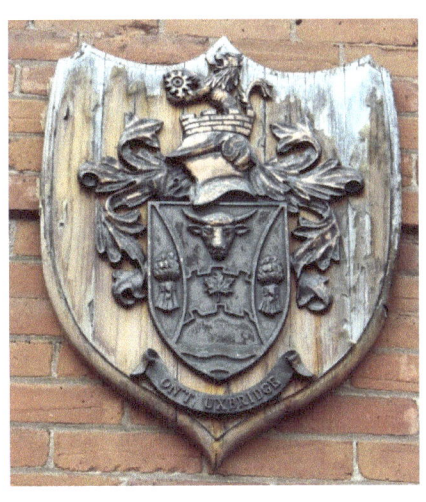

Uxbridge is a township in the Regional Municipality of Durham in south-central Ontario and is located about forty kilometers northeast of Metropolitan Toronto. The main center in the township is the community of Uxbridge. Other communities within the township include Coppins Corners, Goodwood, Leaskdale, Sandford, Siloam, Victoria's Corner, and Zephyr.

It was named for Uxbridge, England, a name which was derived from "Wixan's Bridge".

The first settlers in the area were Quakers who started arriving in 1806 from Pennsylvania. The community's oldest building, the Uxbridge Friends Meeting House, was built in 1820 and overlooks the town from Quaker Hill, a kilometer to the west.

The first passenger-carrying narrow-gauge railway in North America, the Toronto and Nipissing Railway arrived in Uxbridge in June 1871, and for over a decade Uxbridge was the headquarters of the railway. In 1872, the Village of Uxbridge was separated from the Township and incorporated as a separate entity.

With the creation of the Regional Municipality of Durham in 1974, Uxbridge Township was amalgamated with the Town of Uxbridge and Scott Township to create an expanded Township of Uxbridge.

Today, Uxbridge is as a mostly suburban community in northern Durham Region. Major manufacturing employers include Pine Valley Packaging (packaging, containers and portable shelters), Koch-Glitsch Canada (mass transfer systems) and Hela Canada (spice and ingredient manufacture). Many residents commute to other centers in Durham and York Regions and beyond.

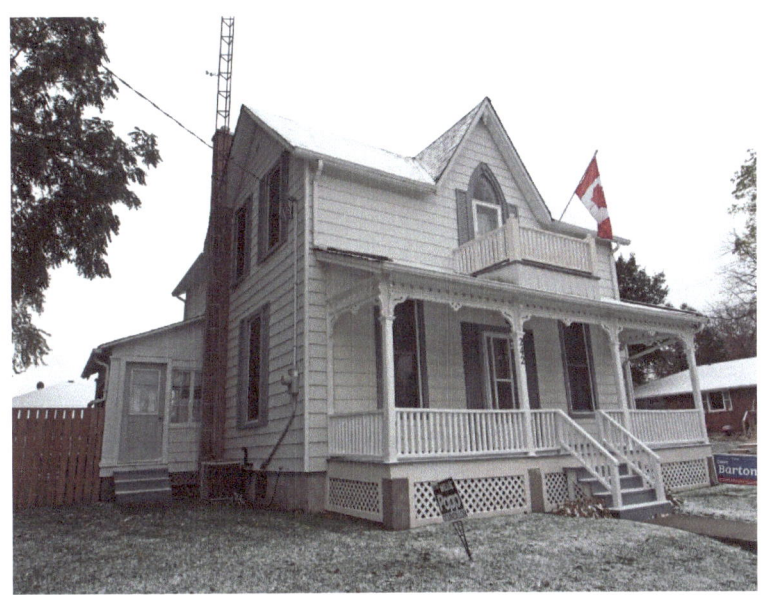

242 Brock Street West – Gothic Revival

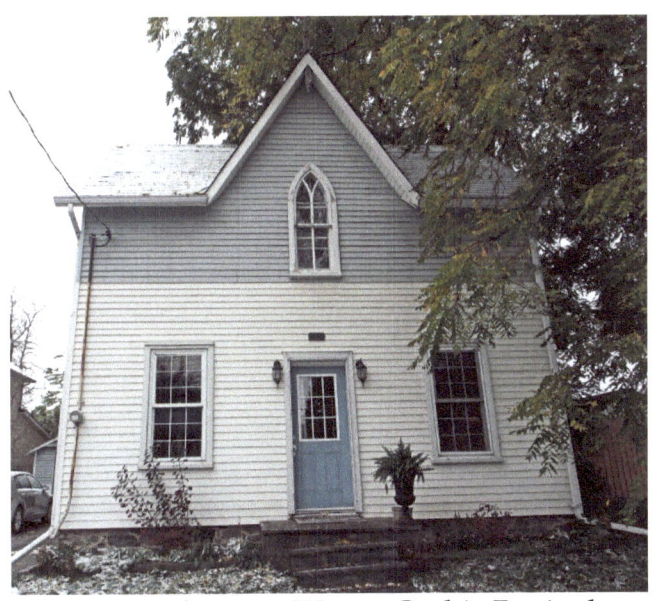

236 Brock Street West – Gothic Revival

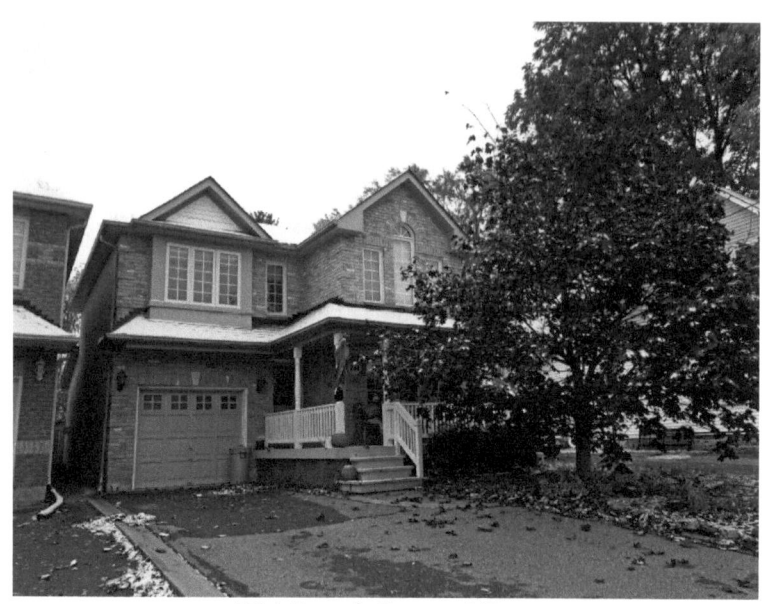

234 Brock Street West

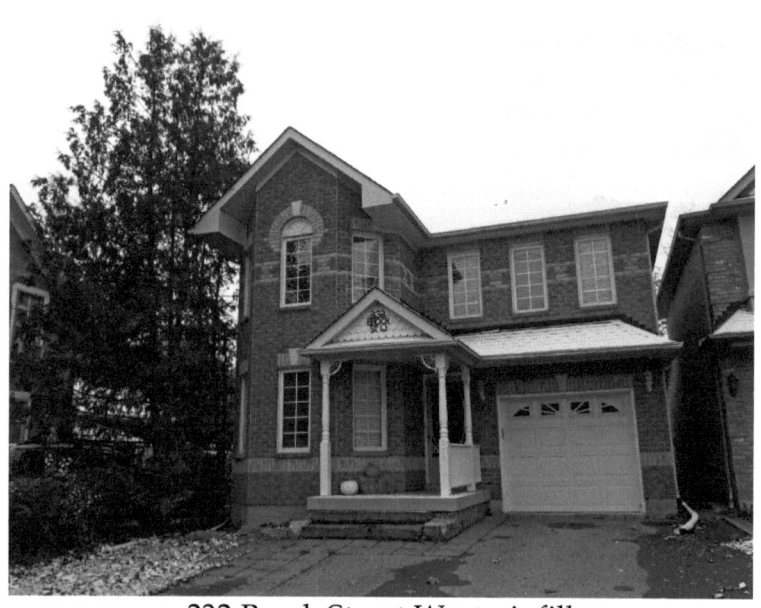

232 Brock Street West - infill

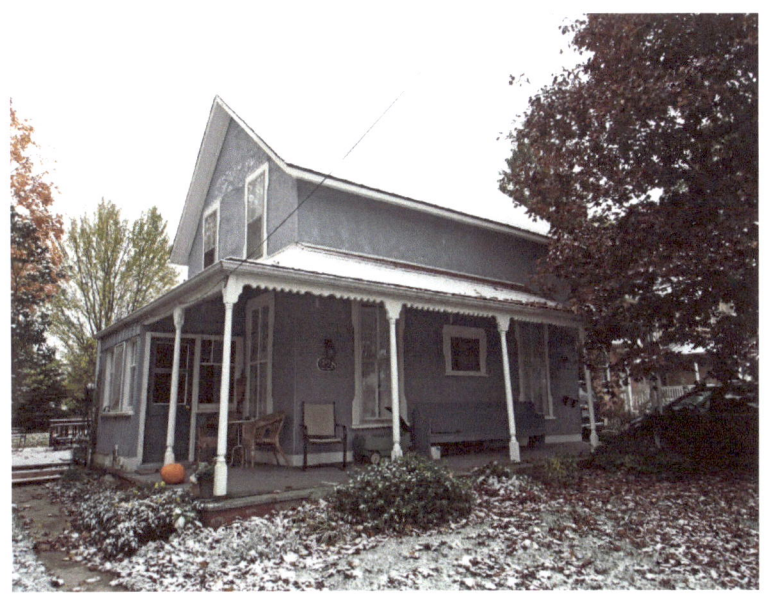

228 Brock Street West

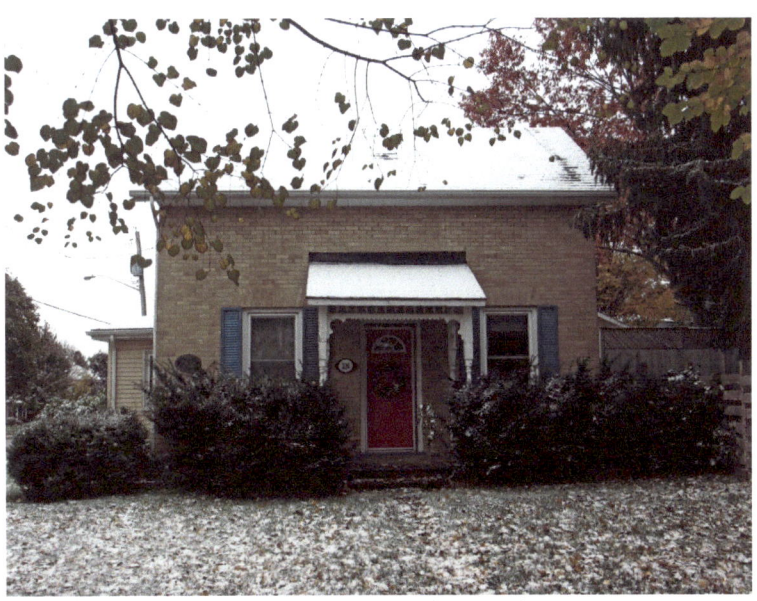

220 Brock Street West – John and Elizabeth Nevison House – c. 1876 – Harness Maker

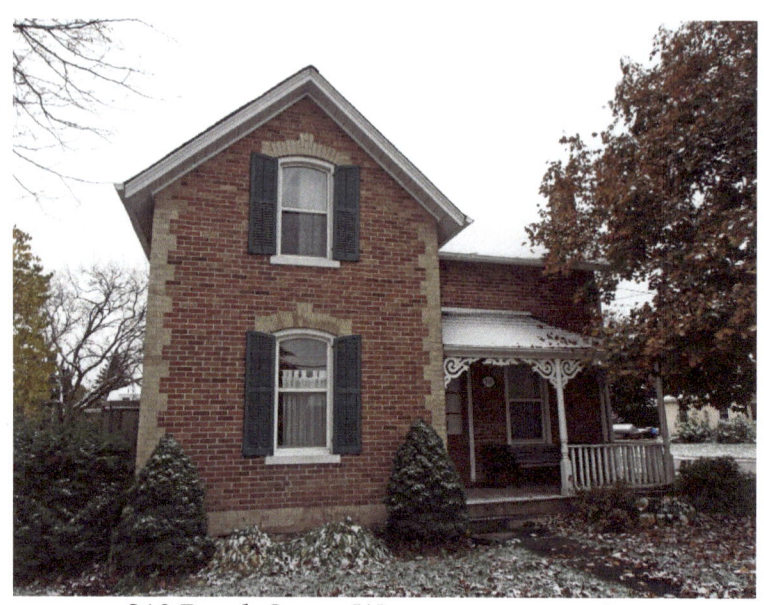

210 Brock Street West – corner quoins

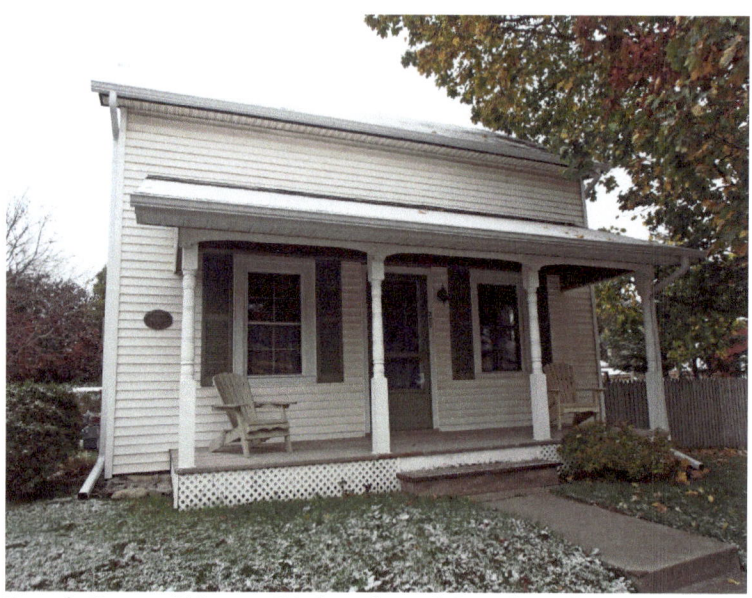

209 Brock Street West – Richard and Sarah Sellers House – c. 1856 – Labourer

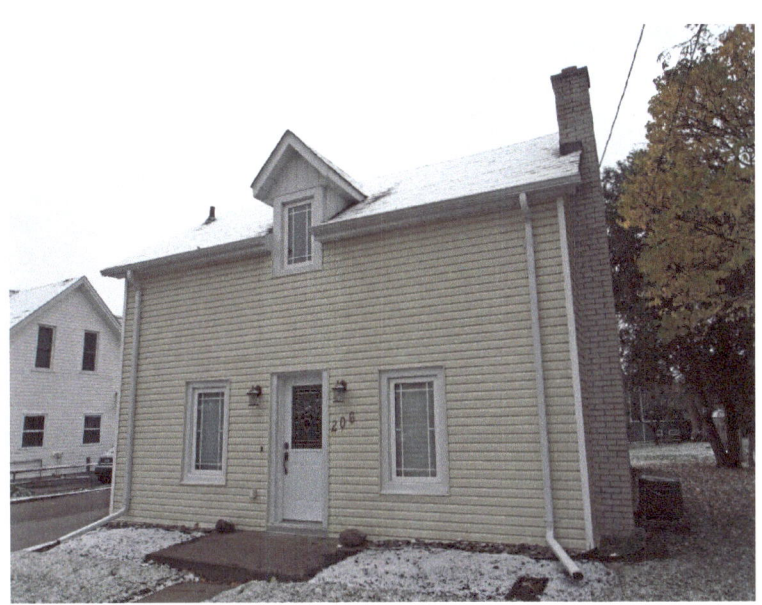

206 Brock Street West - dormer

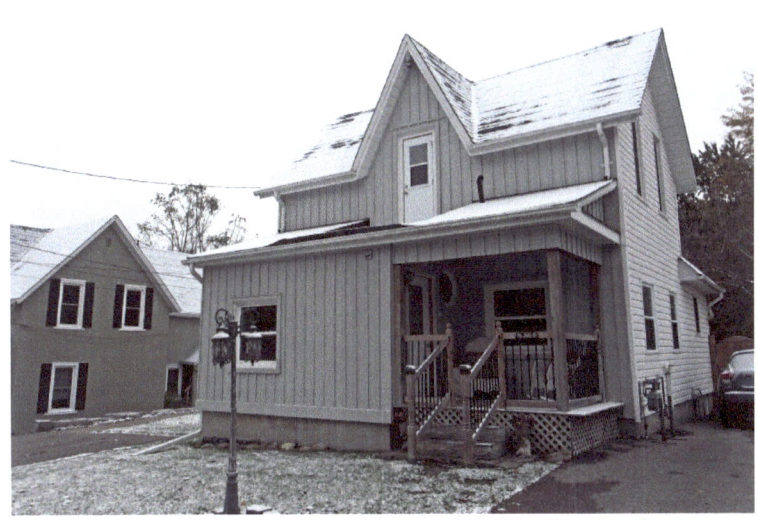

200 Brock Street West – Gothic Revival

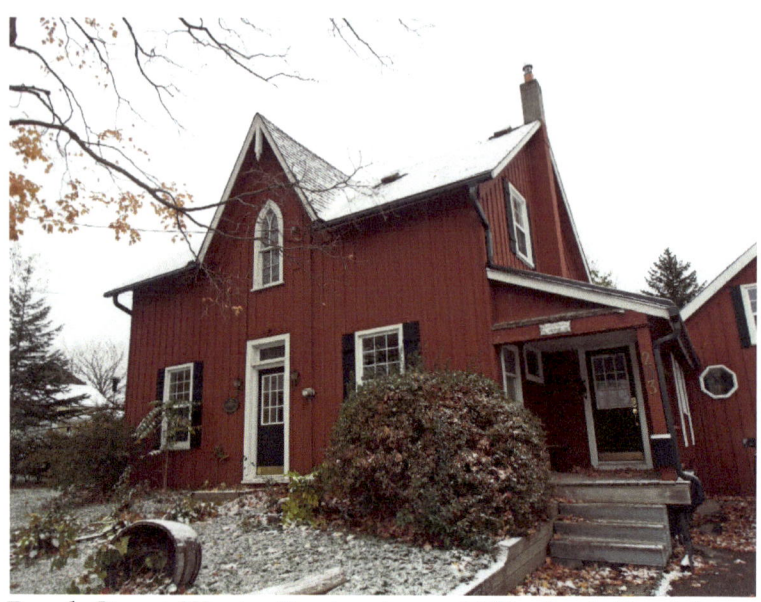

203 Brock Street West – Benjamin and Elizabeth Davidson House – c. 1866 – Manufacturer and Bee Keeper – Gothic Revival with finial on gable

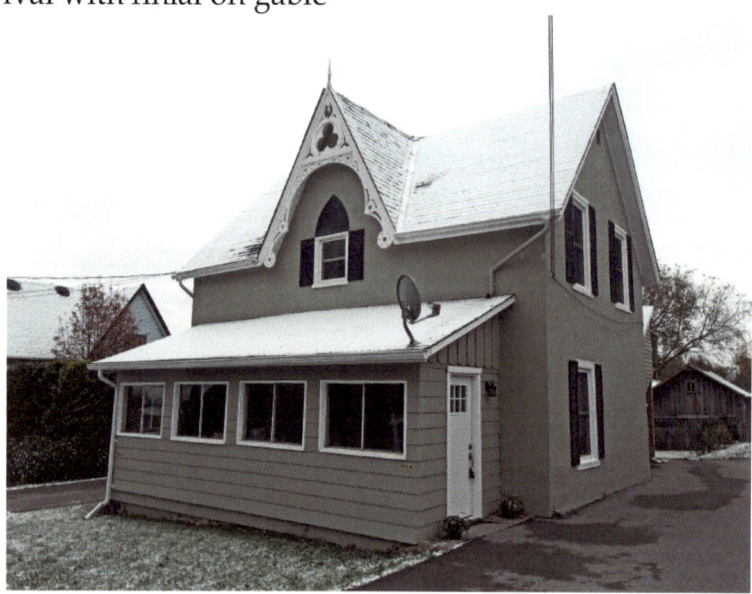

194 Brock Street West – Gothic Revival with verge board trim and finial on gable

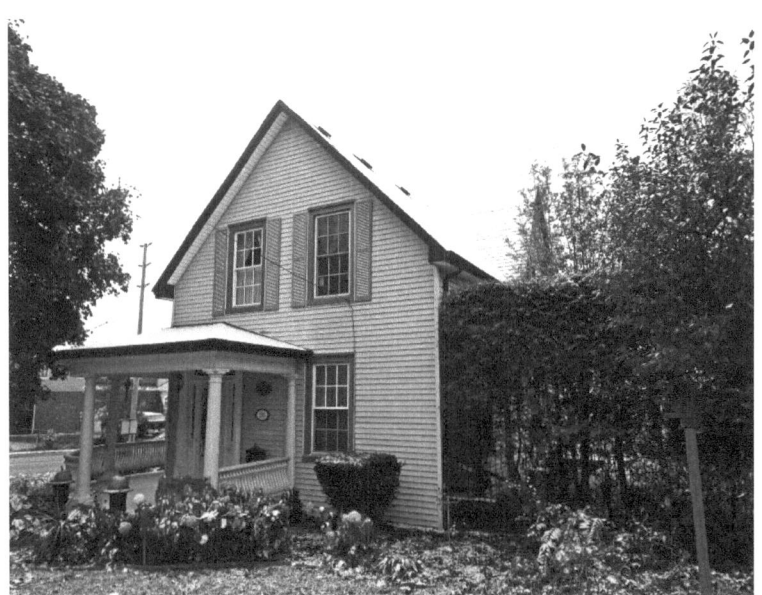

188 Brock Street West – Boyd House – 1½ story house built in 1876-77 with wrap around verandah. Gable on second floor has a door that opens onto a railed verandah. It still has the original six over six windows and has a fieldstone foundation.

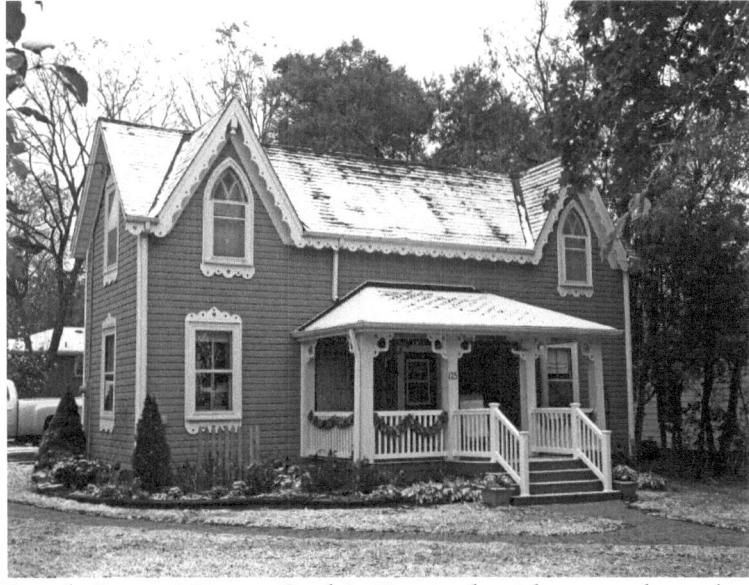

175 Brock Street West – Gothic Revival with verge board trim on gable

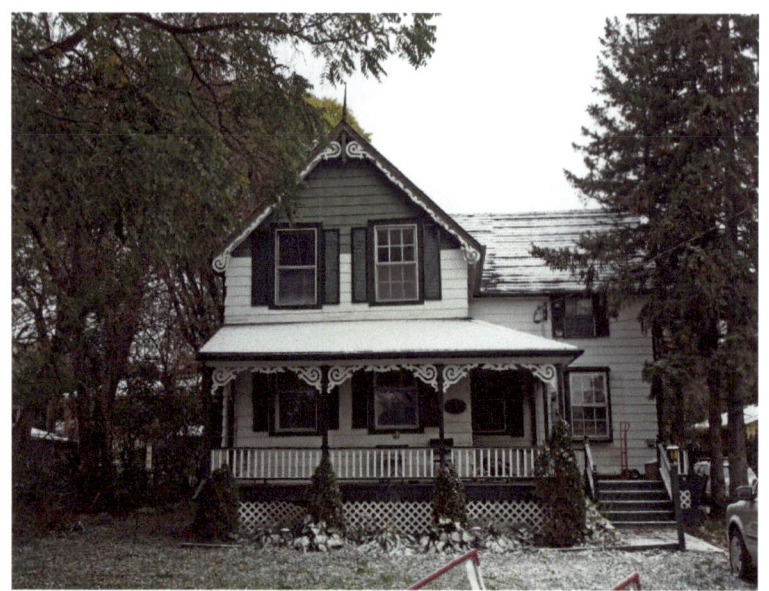

169 Brock Street West – Jones House – Town Constable – c. 1876 – Gothic Revival with verge board trim and finial on gable

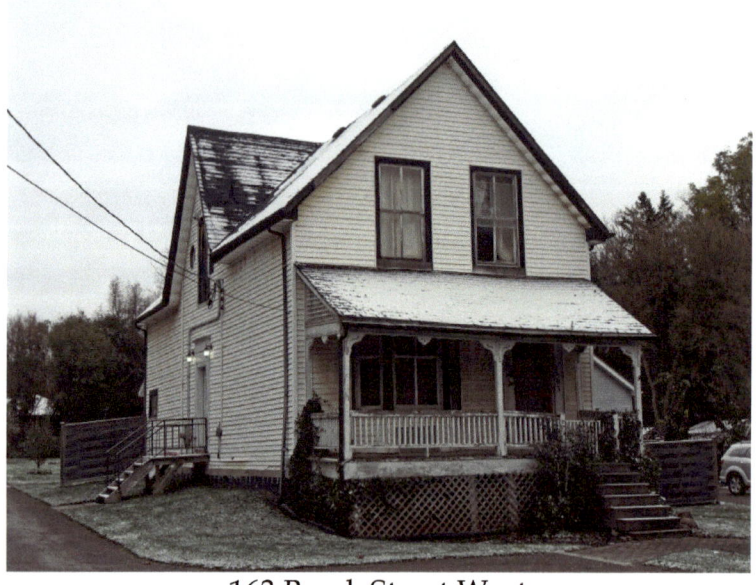

163 Brock Street West

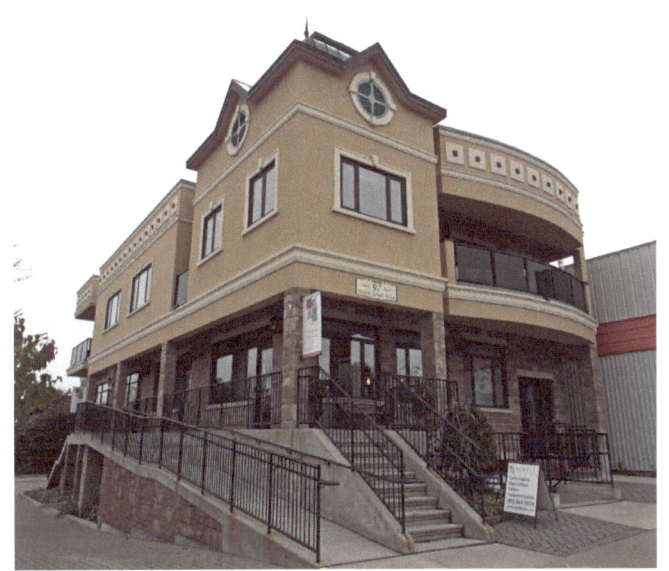

97 Brock Street West

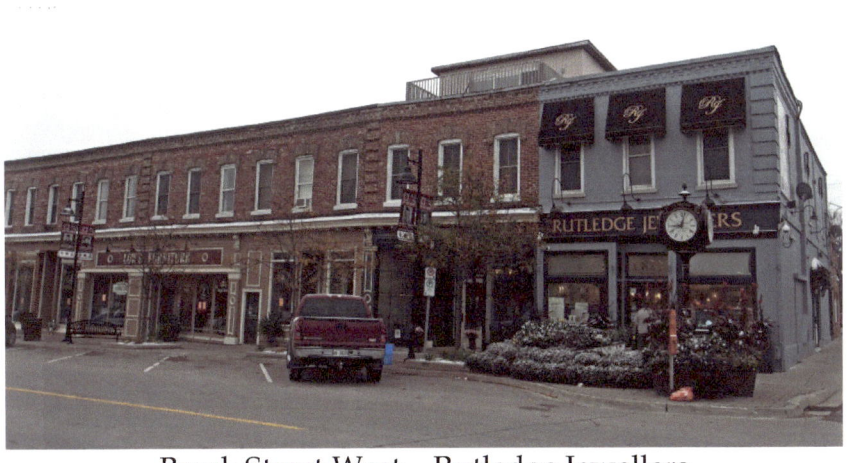

Brock Street West – Rutledge Jewellers

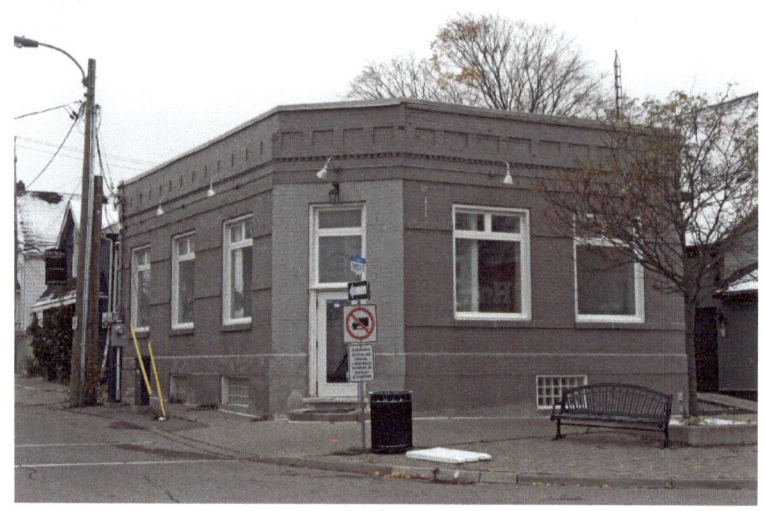

96 Brock Street West

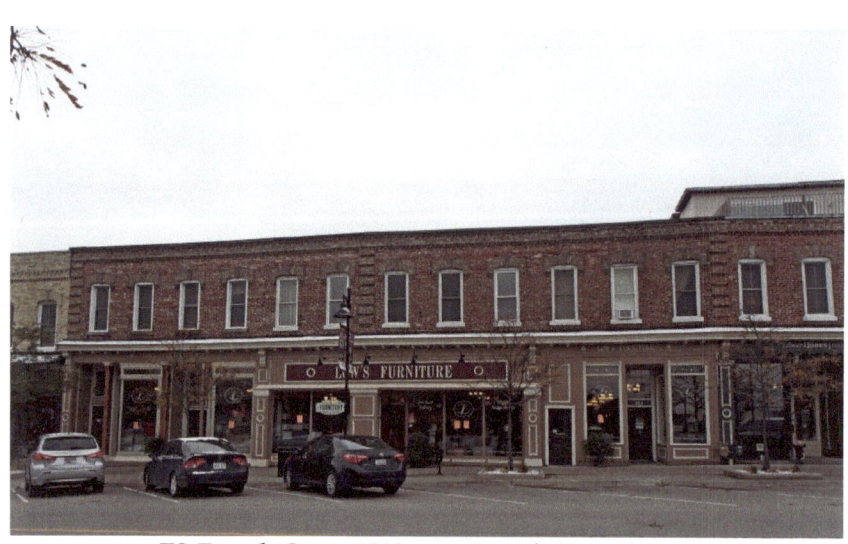

78 Brock Street West – Low's Furniture

66-70 Brock Street West – The Passionate Cook's Bistro and Fine Food & Cheese Shop

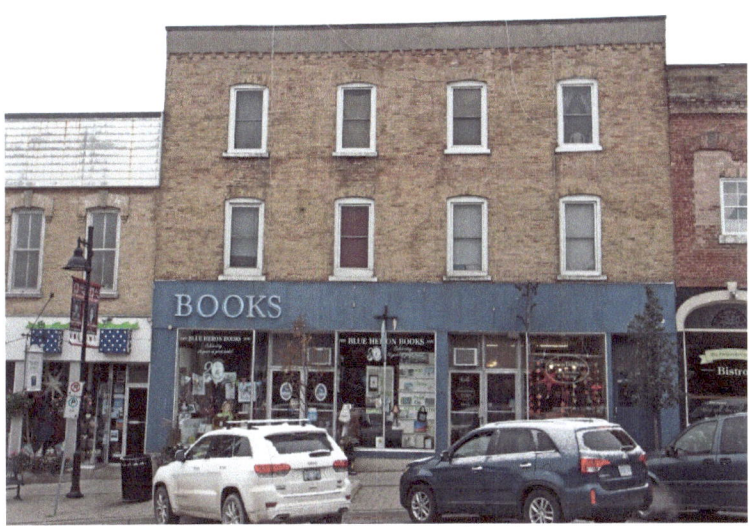

64 Brock Street West – book store

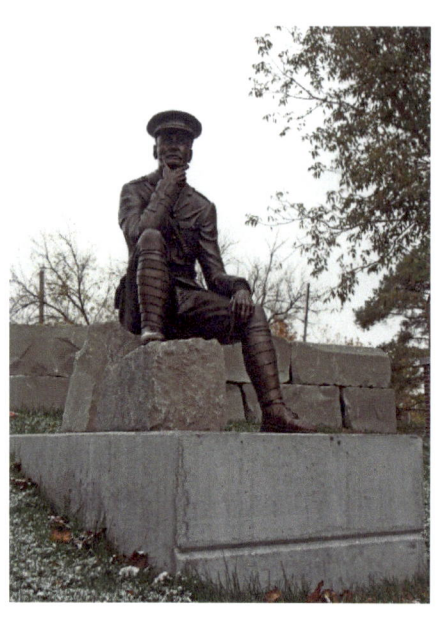

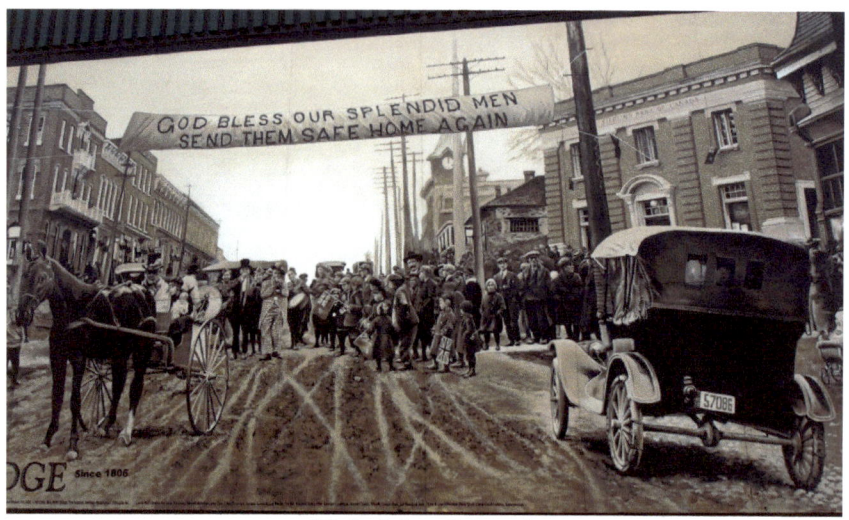

Uxbridge Mural

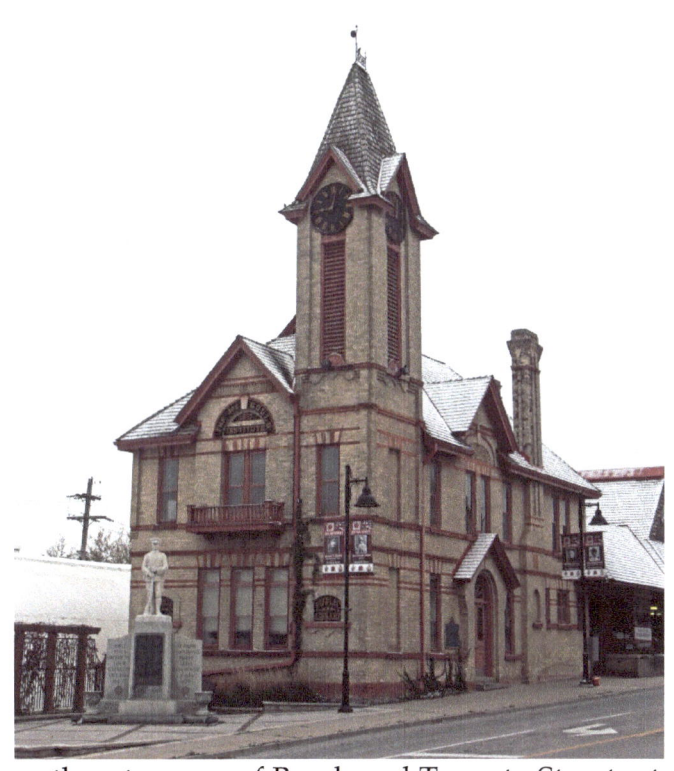

At the southeast corner of Brock and Toronto Streets stands the Uxbridge Public Library (c. 1887). It was beautifully restored in 1985. Uxbridge's citizen, Joseph Gould, commissioned it as a Mechanics' Institute and John T. Stokes of Sharon was the probable architect. It is in the High Victorian Gothic style of architecture which is reflected in its picturesque roofline, impressive clock tower and lavish attention to detail such as projecting brick courses, buttresses, bricks set in a diagonal pattern, decorative red brick, ornate chimneys and dropped brick keystones over the windows.

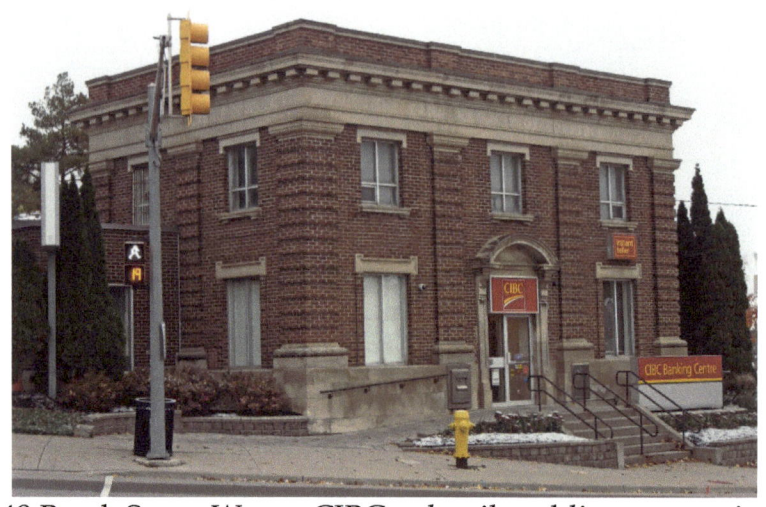

49 Brock Street West – CIBC – dentil molding, voussoirs

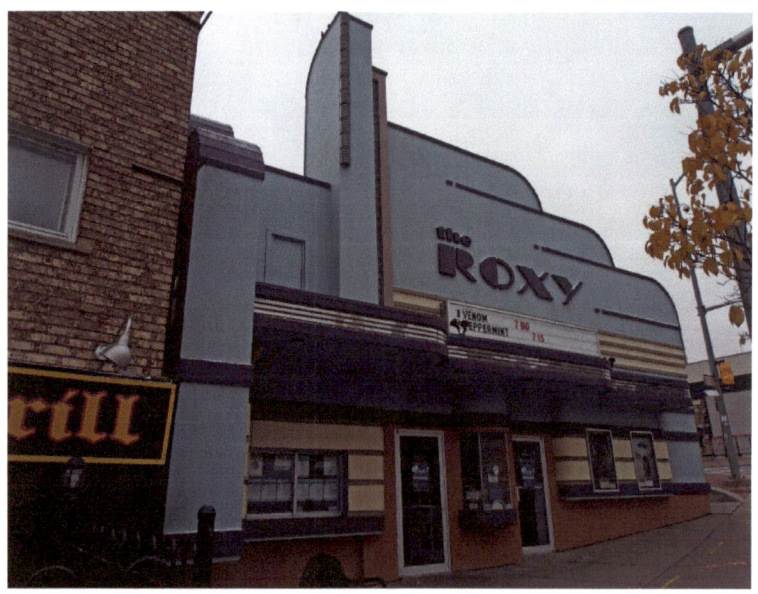

Brock Street West – The Roxy Theatre

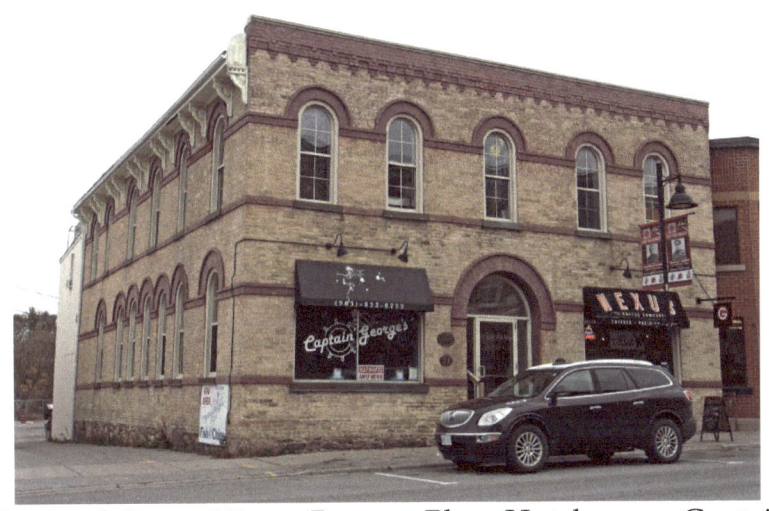

19-21 Brock Street West – Bascom Place Hotel – now Captain George's Fish 'n' Chips

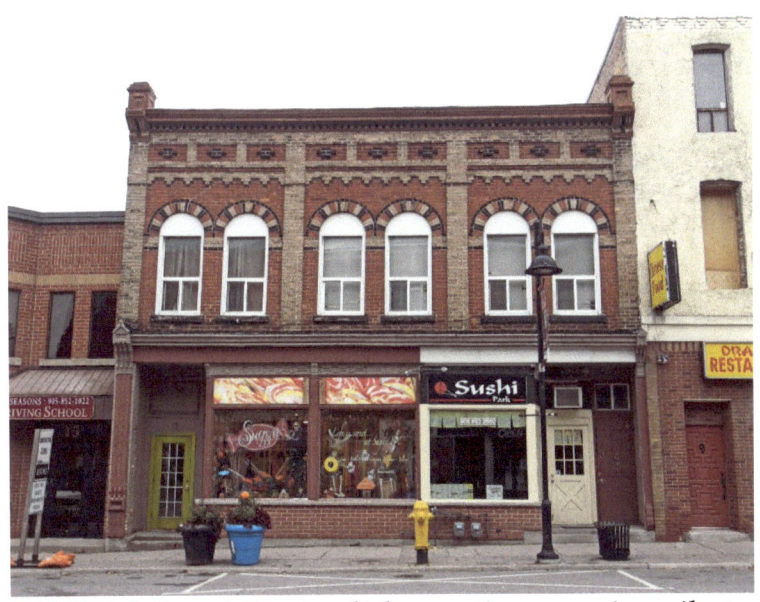

11-13 Brock Street West – dichromatic voussoirs, pilasters

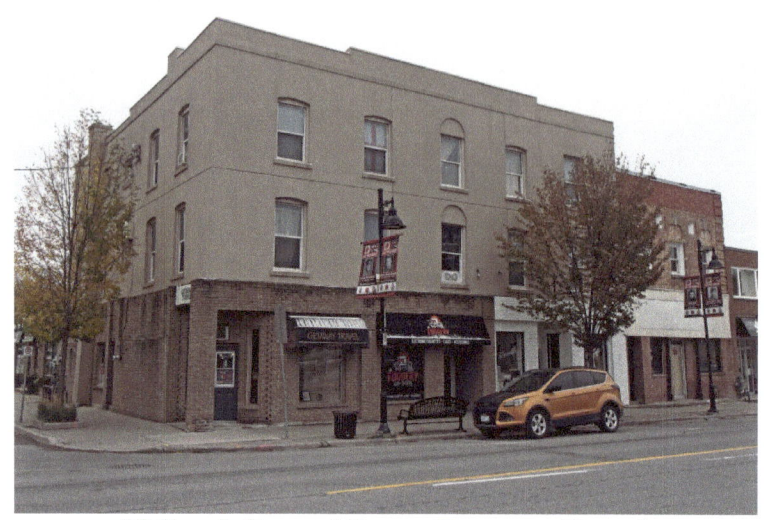

22 Brock Street West – Getaway Travel

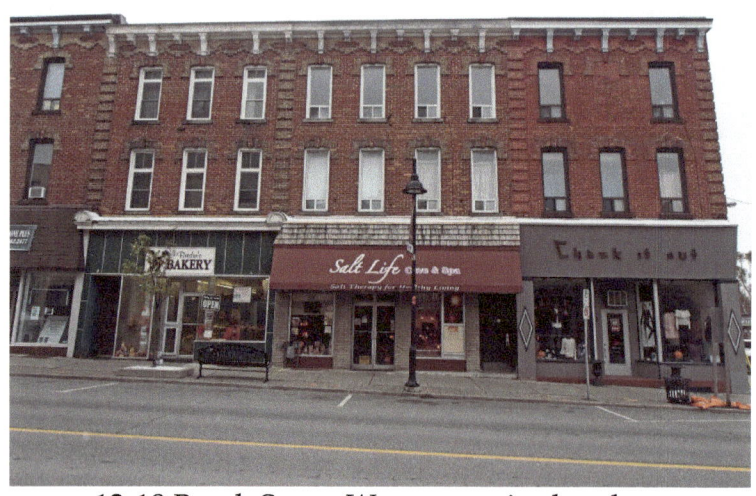

12-18 Brock Street West – cornice brackets

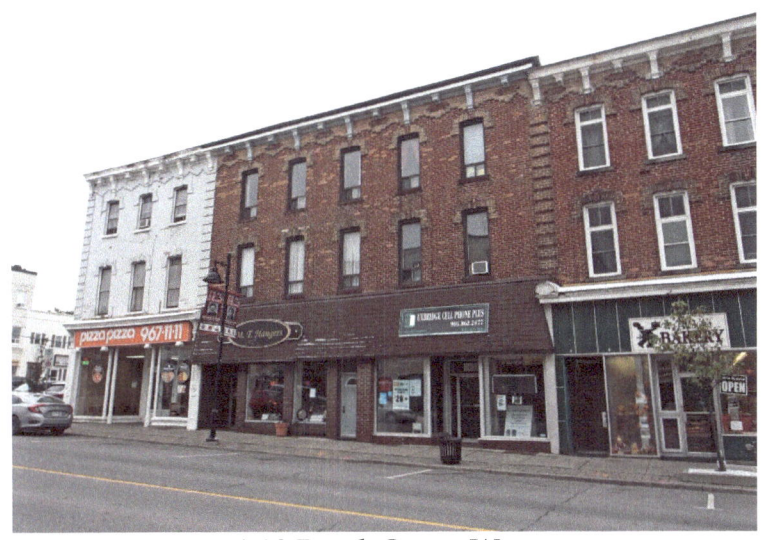

6-10 Brock Street West

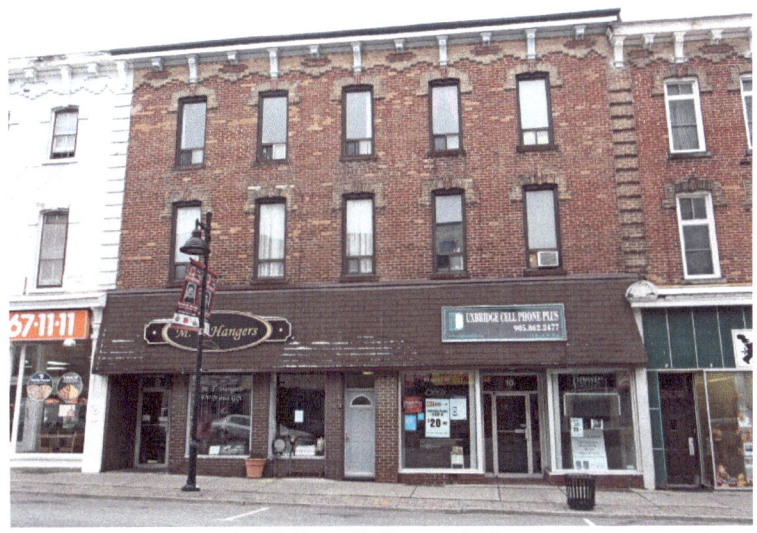

8-10 Brock Street West

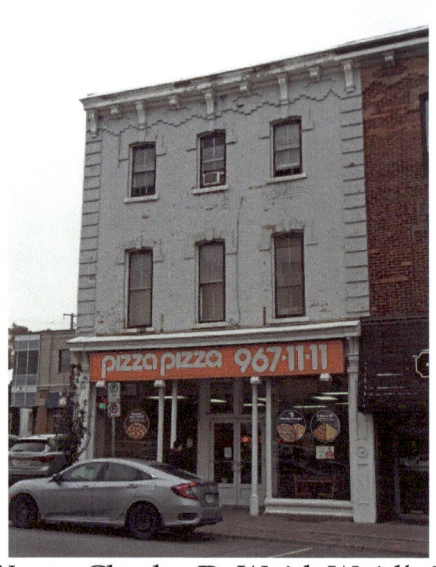

6 Brock Street West – Charles D. Waid, Waid's Jewelry Store - now Pizza Pizza

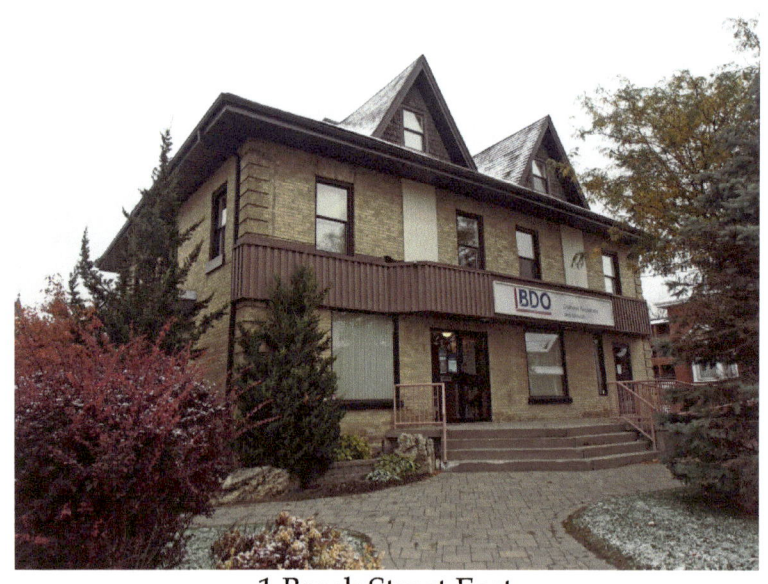

1 Brock Street East

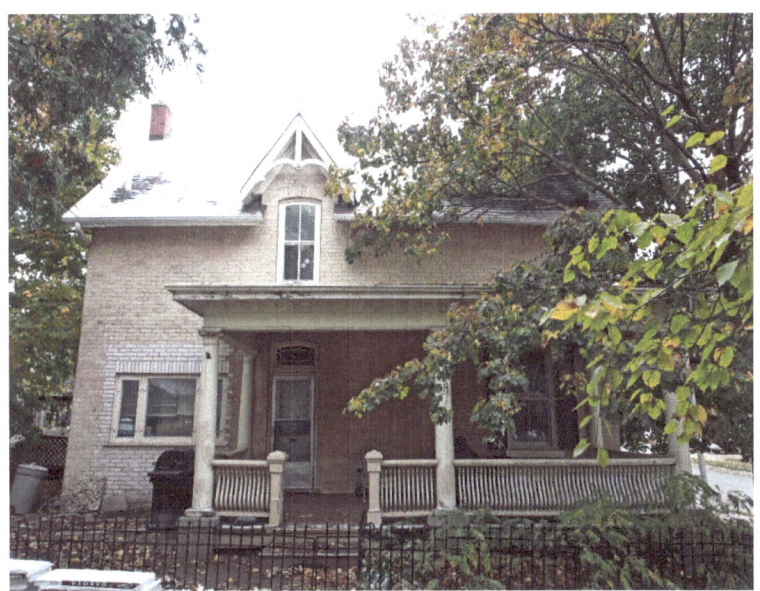

7 Brock Street East – finial and trim on gable

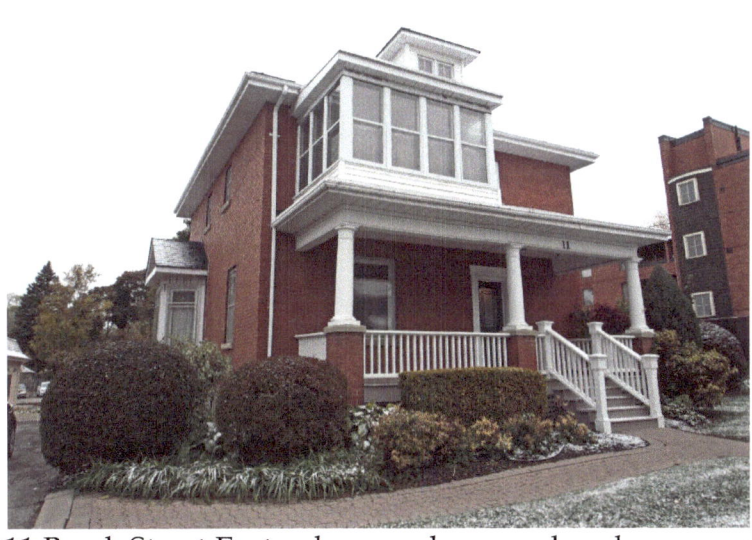

11 Brock Street East – dormer above enclosed sunroom

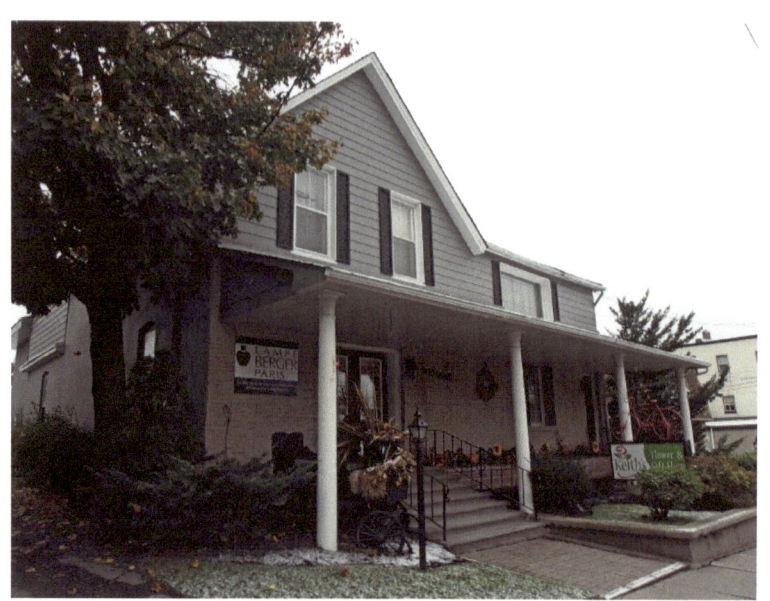
14 Brock Street East

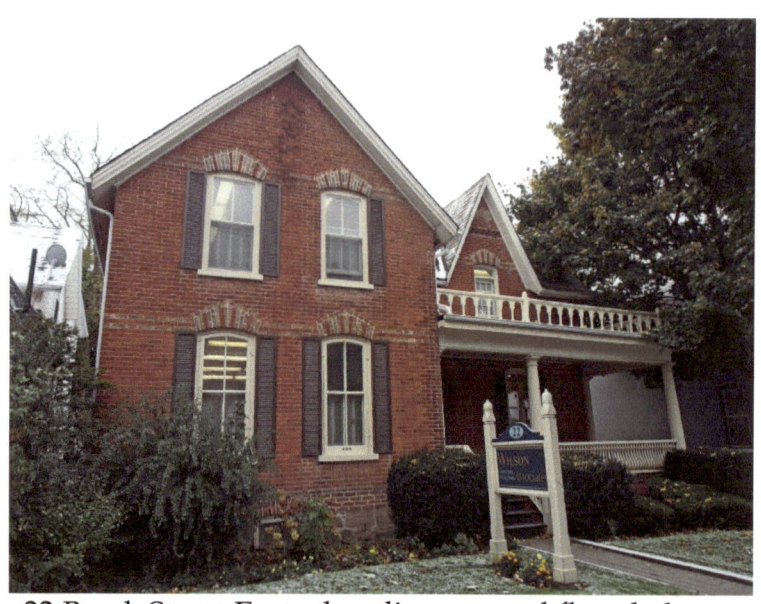
22 Brock Street East – banding, second floor balcony

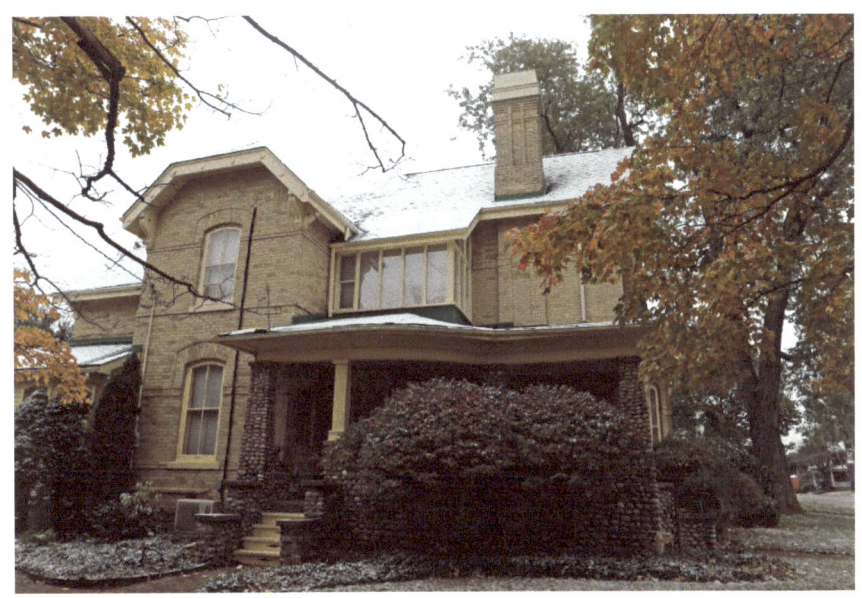

35 Brock Street East - patterning in gable, decorative cornice and brackets, arched windows and voussoirs, banding

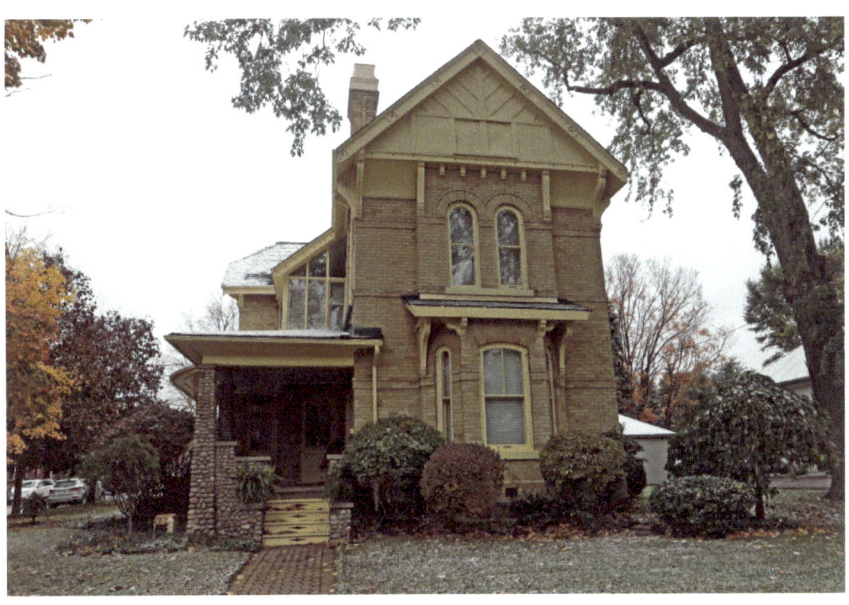

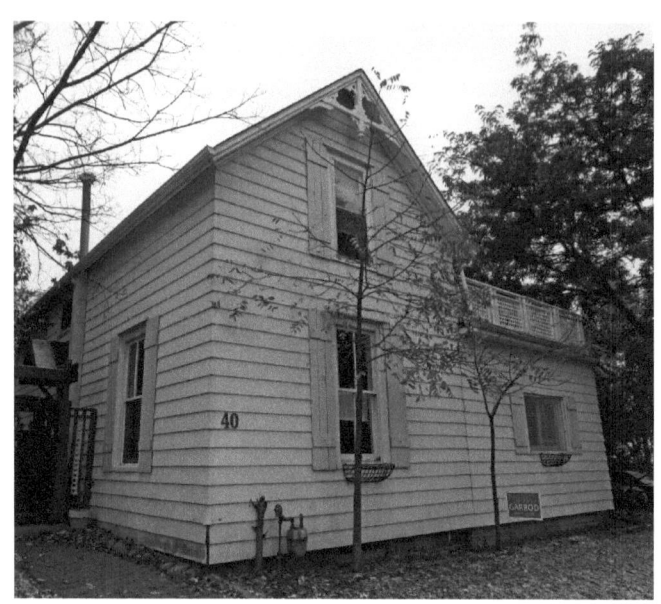

40 Brock Street East

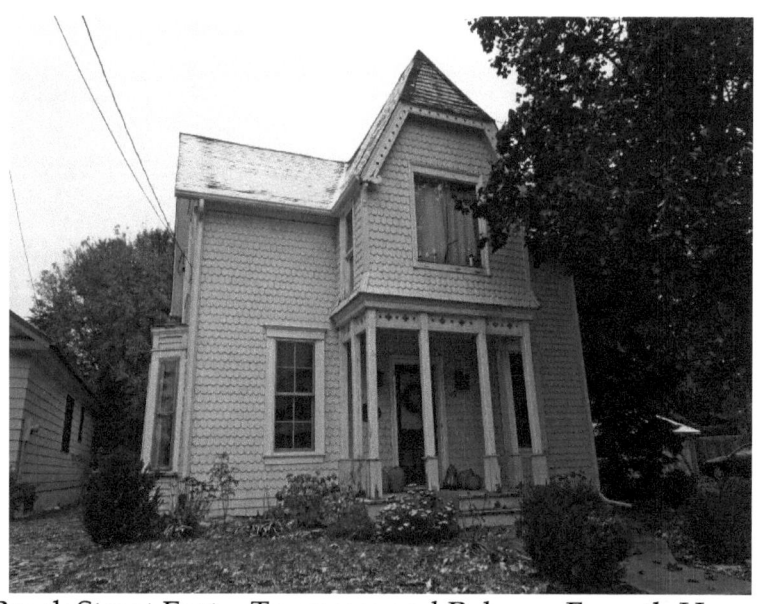

45 Brock Street East – Trumann and Rebecca Forsyth House – c. 1872 – Pump Maker

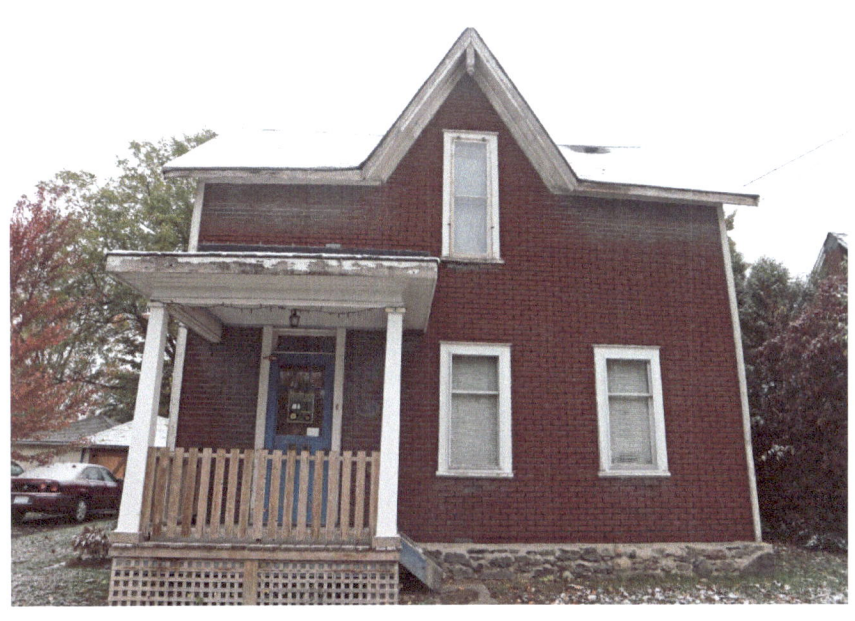

51 Brock Street East – Baptist Parsonage (1924-1963) – c. 1862

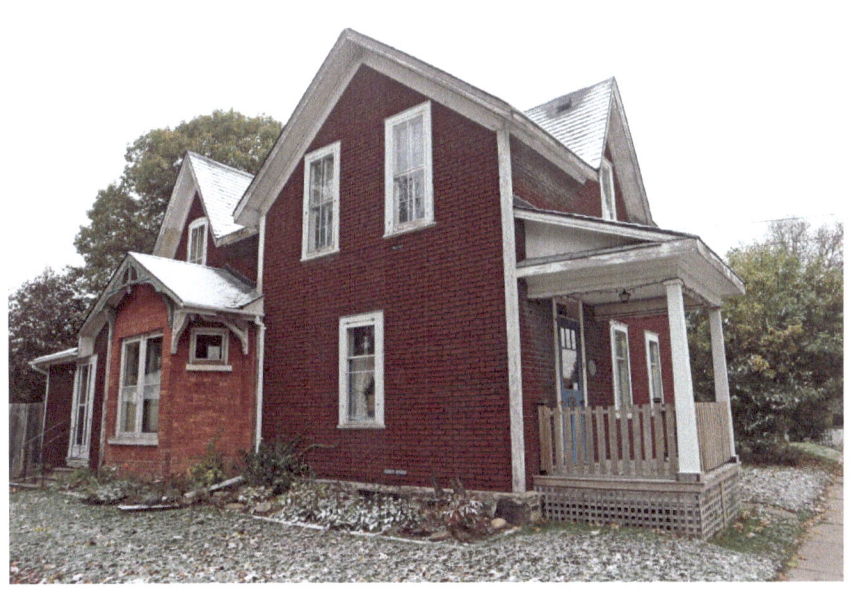

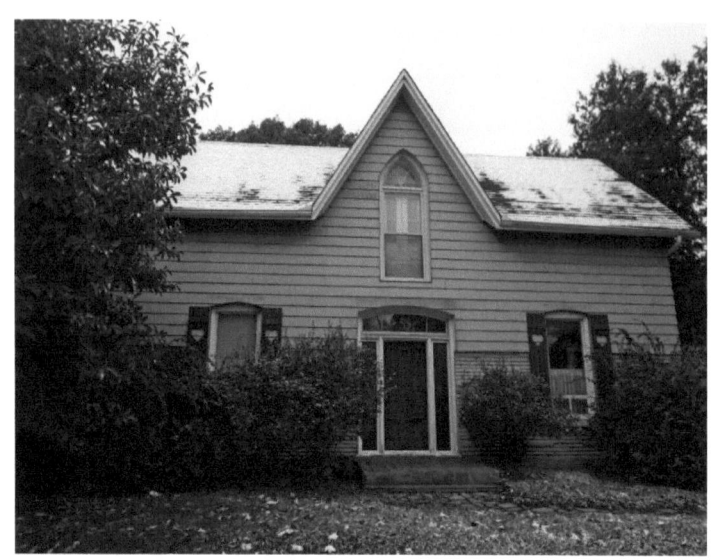

55 Brock Street East - Harrison House - The 1½ story home with back kitchen and dining room was built in 1873 by Henry Madill Jr. who operated a dry goods store on Brock Street. James Harrison, a harness maker on Main Street for twenty years, purchased it in 1861. From 1949-1950, Mrs. Alma Soper used it as Cedarlea Maternity Home.

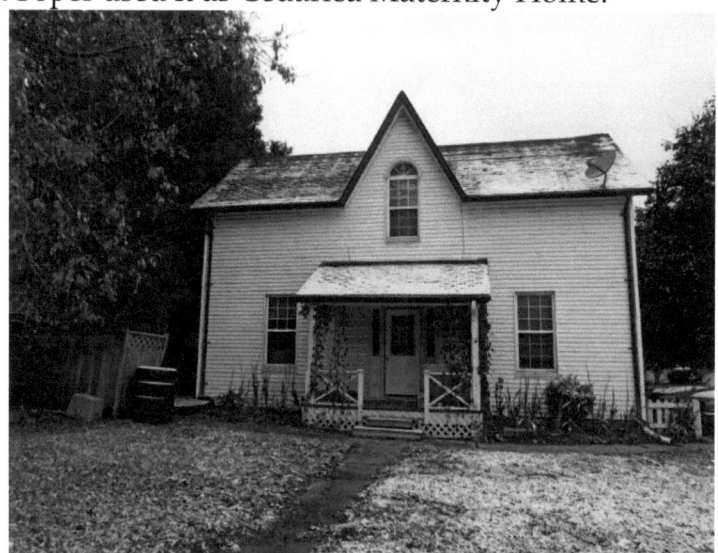

61 Brock Street East

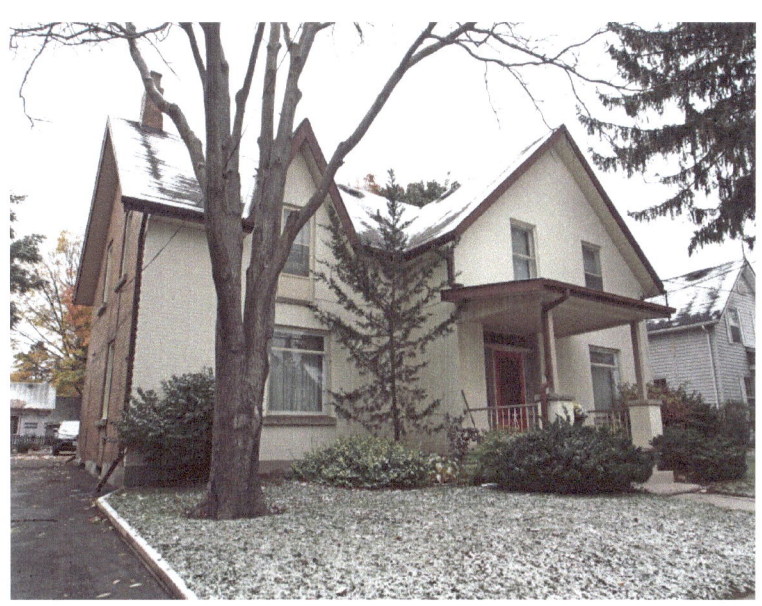

56 Brock Street East

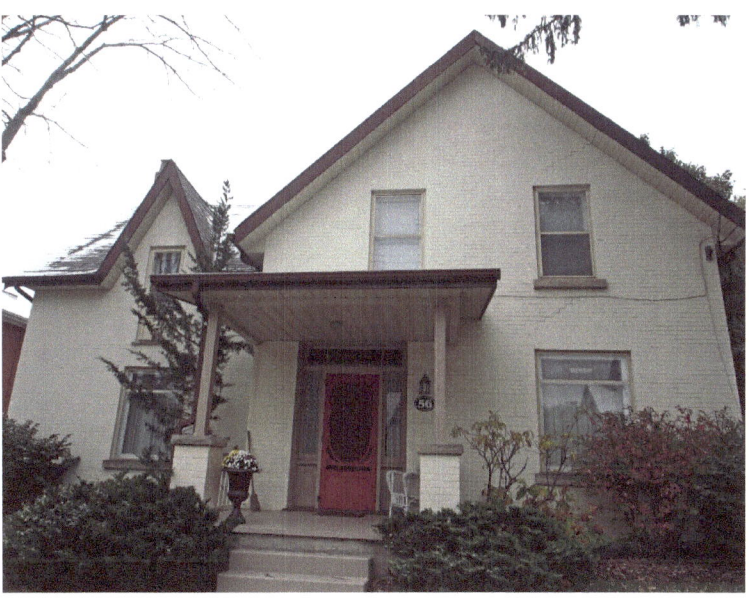

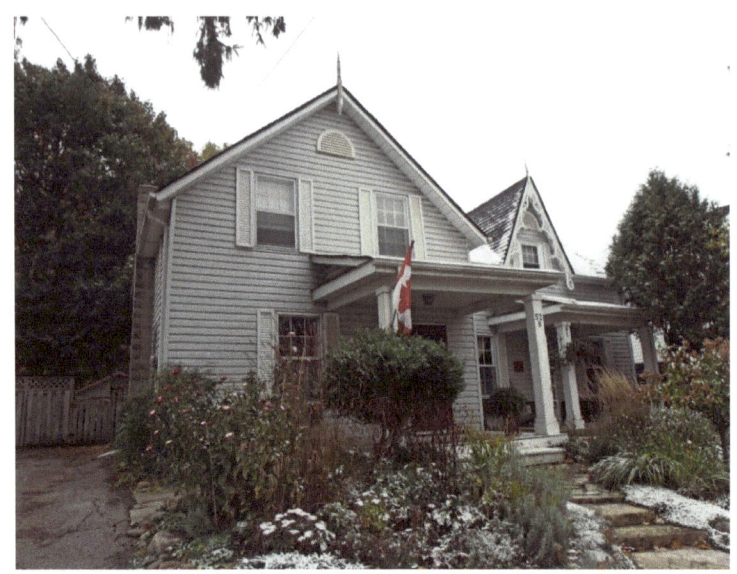

52 Brock Street East

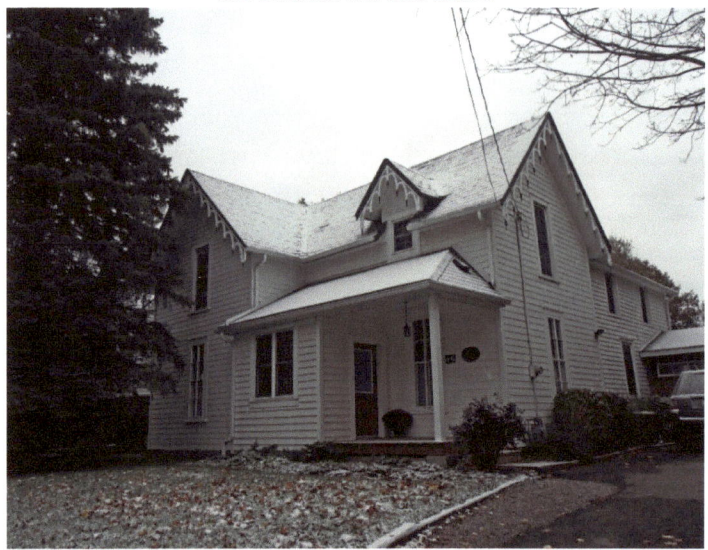

46 Brock Street East – Harman House – c. 1869 – Teacher - R.P. Harman House - Gothic Revival 1½ story frame house with gables was sold to A.T. Button who was a merchant and lumber dealer. It has a fieldstone foundation; windows are 6 over 6 and 2 over 2; and it has original door - gingerbread trim along the gables.

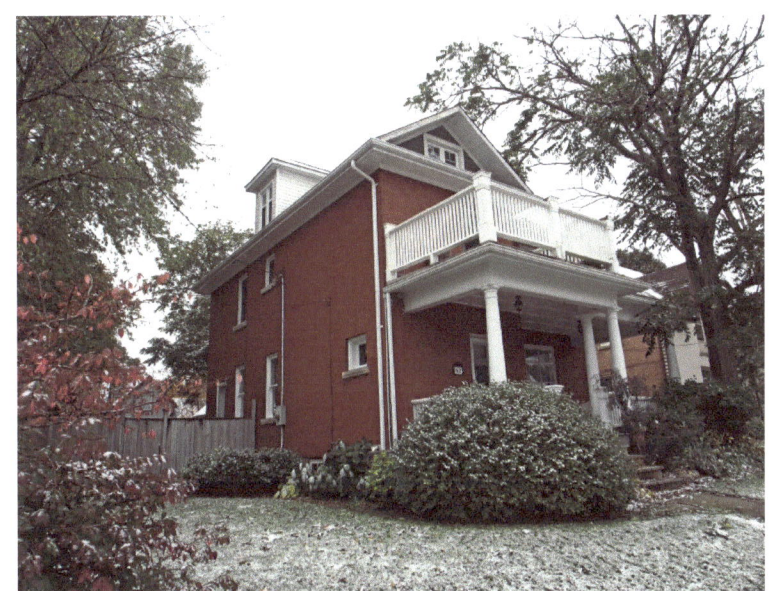

62 Brock Street East

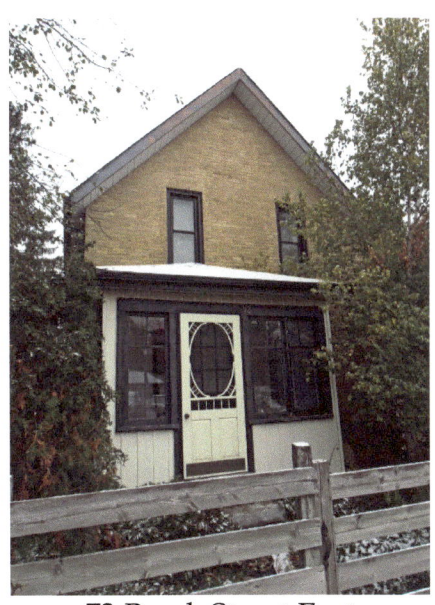

73 Brock Street East

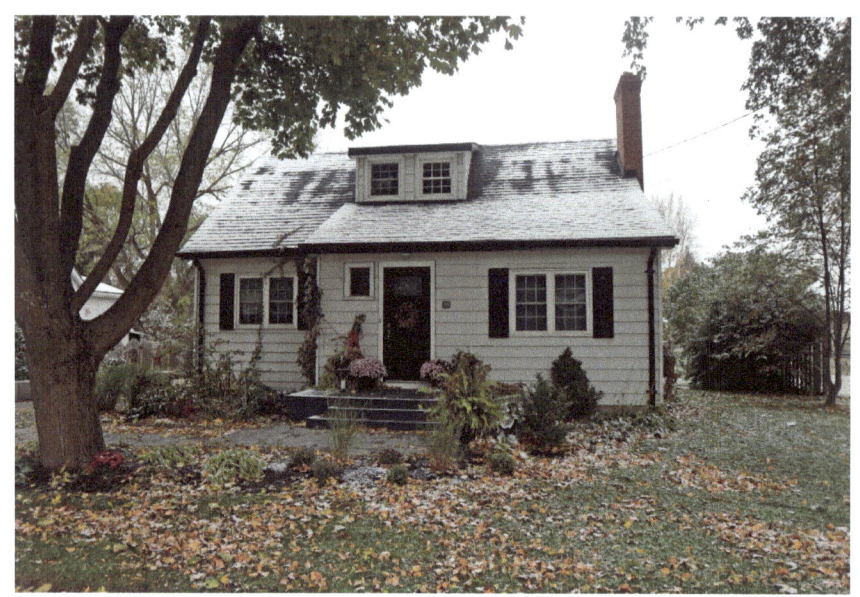

95 Brock Street East

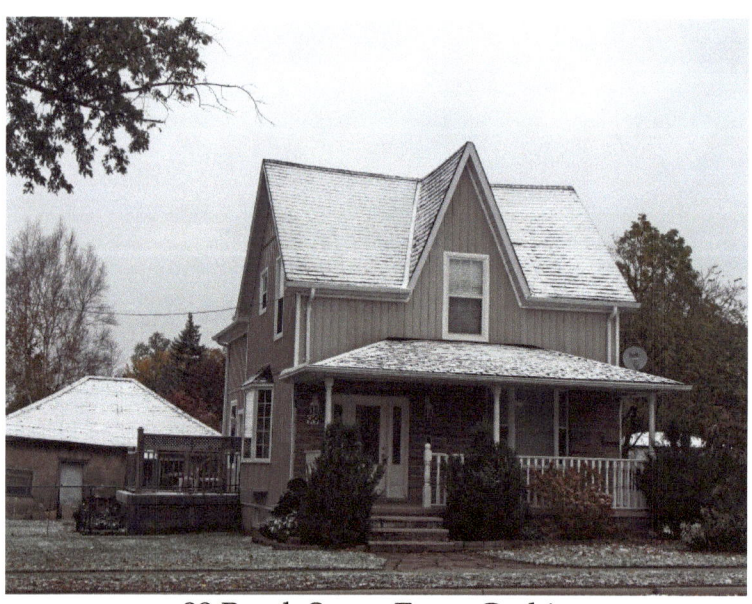

99 Brock Street East - Gothic

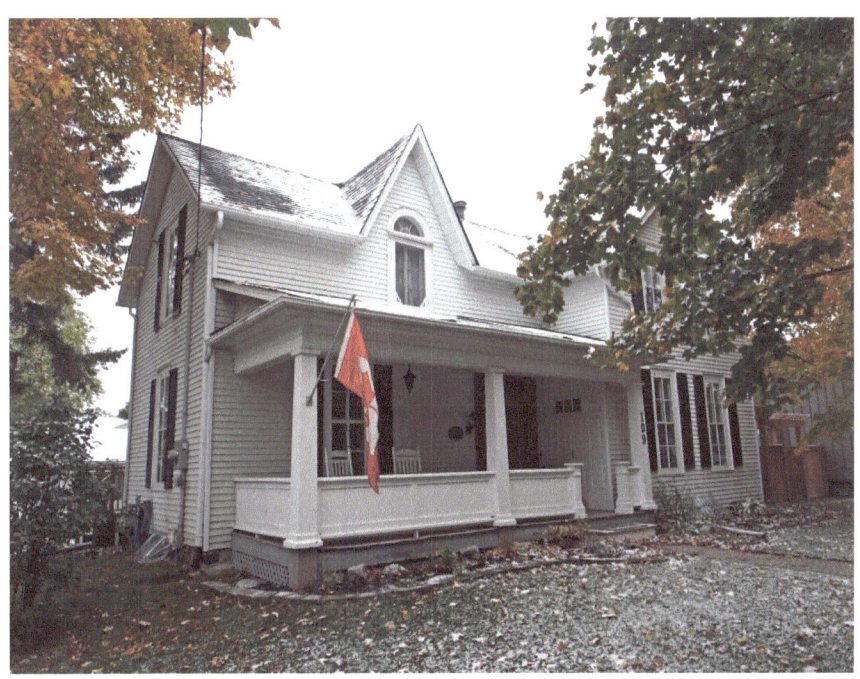

109 Brock Street East - R.P. Harman House – c. 1871 – This L-shaped, 1½ story frame house with large and small gables has a Gothic style door which opens onto a small railed verandah. Stained glass sidelights and transom around the front door are features of this house. Reuben P. Harman was a school teacher and businessman. He owned Sash and Door Factory.

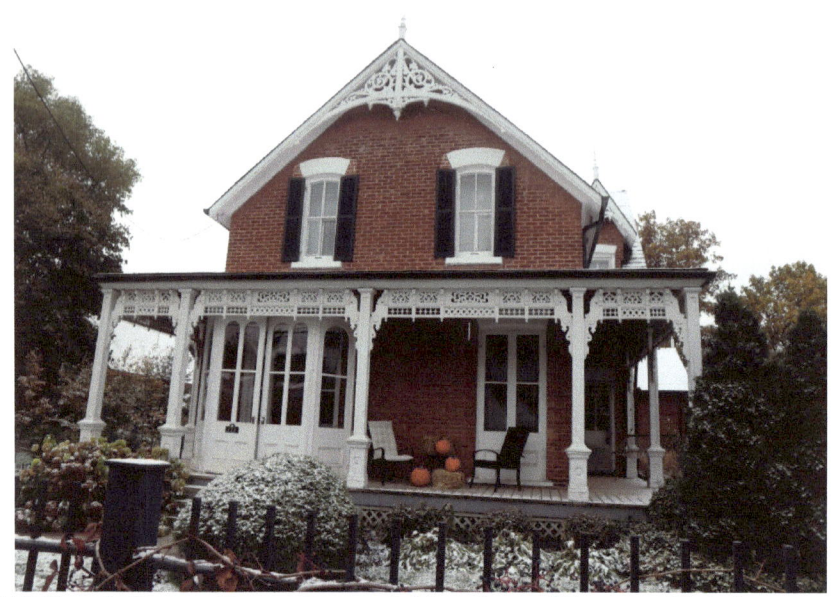

112 Brock Street East - Samuel Umphrey House - This house was built in 1871 by Samuel Umphrey, a prominent Uxbridge Businessman, who played an important role in the Uxbridge Cabinet Organ Factory. This Victorian house has a fine example of bargeboard, spool work and fretwork.

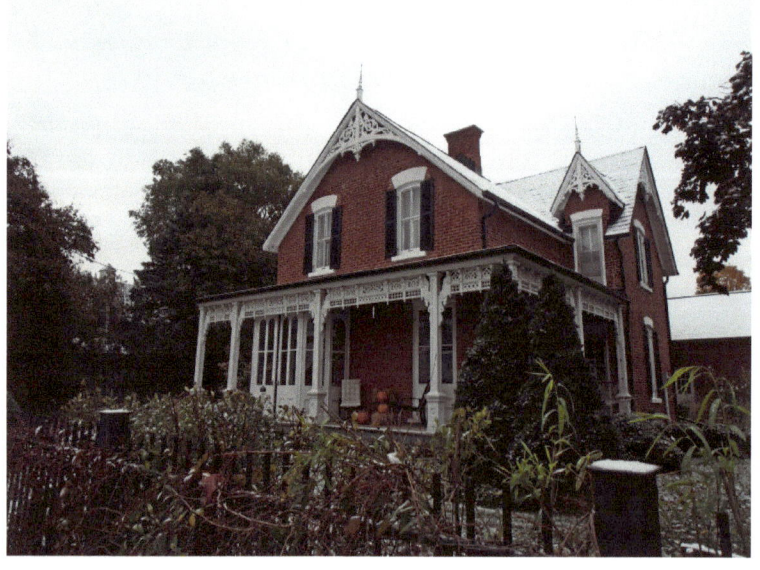

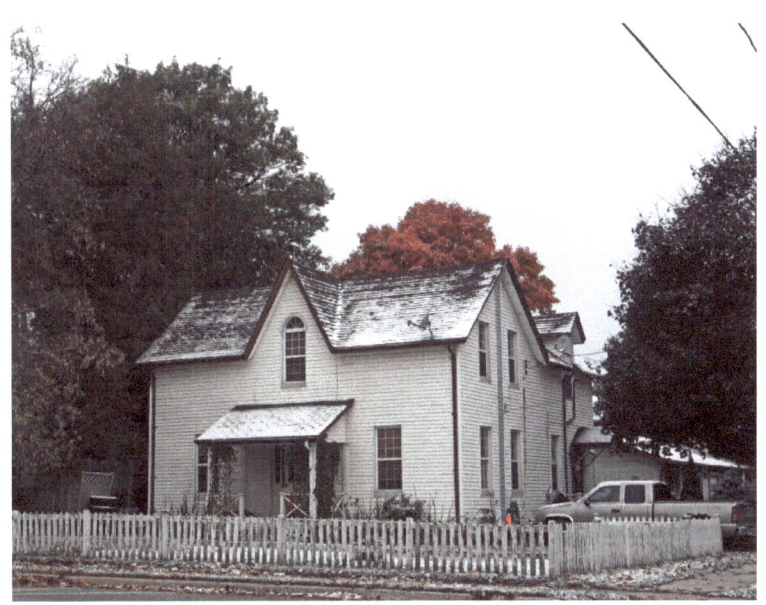

Brock Street East – Gothic

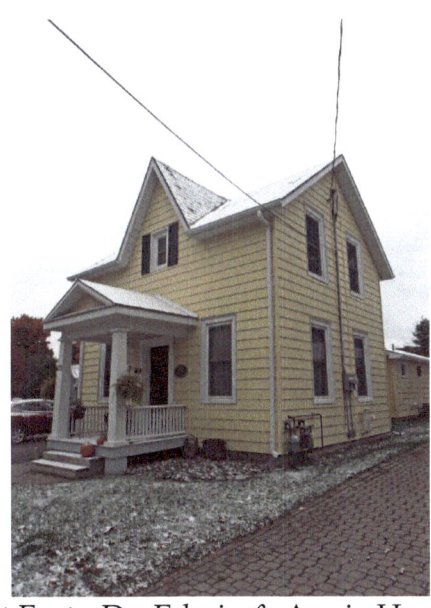

130 Brock Street East - Dr. Edwin & Annie Hardy House, Educator, O.B.E. – c. 1895

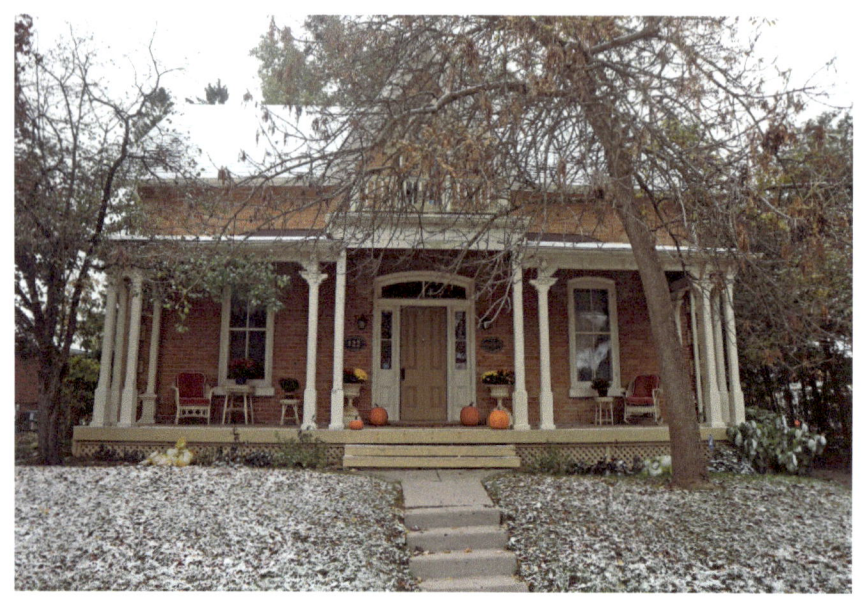

122 Brock Street East - Robert & Elizabeth Mooney House, Merchant – c. 1874 – Gothic - corner quoins

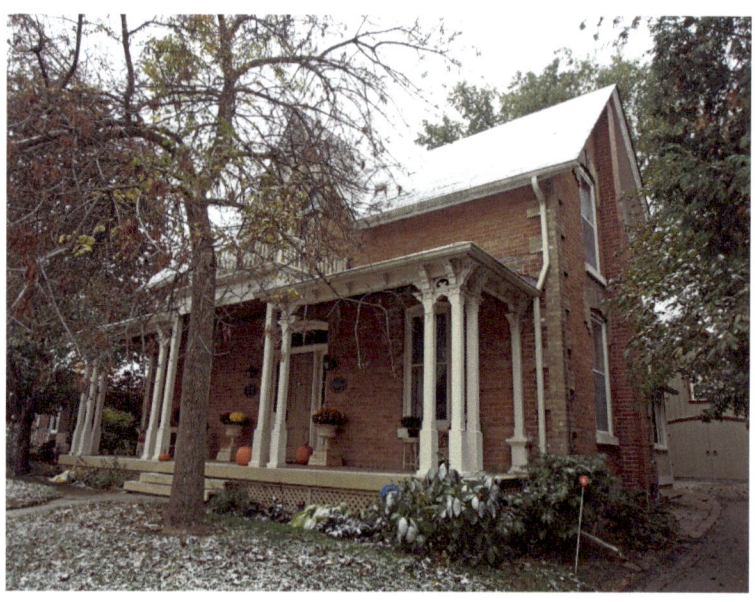

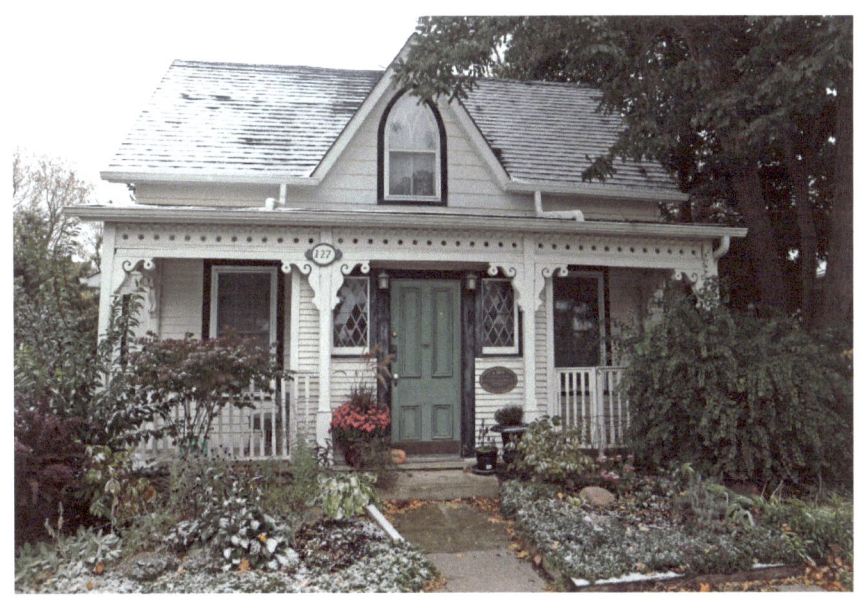

127 Brock Street East - Benjamin & Elizabeth Clemence House, Shoemaker – c. 1879 - Gothic

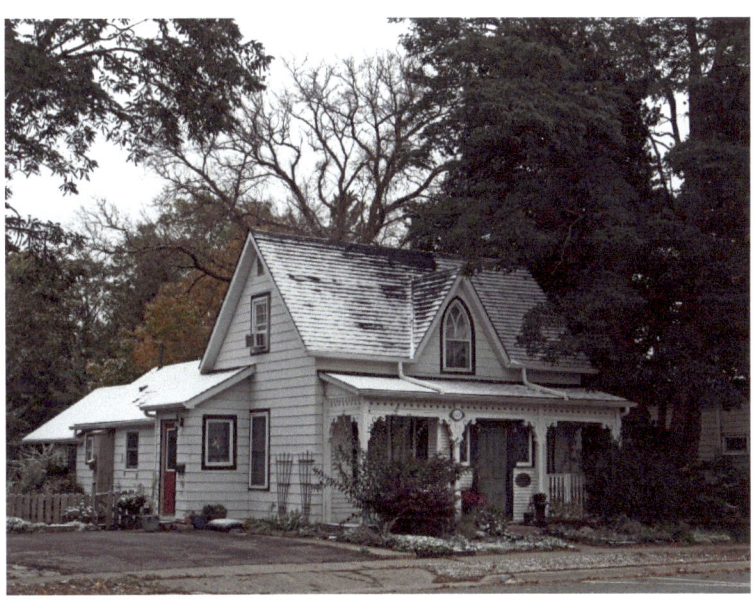

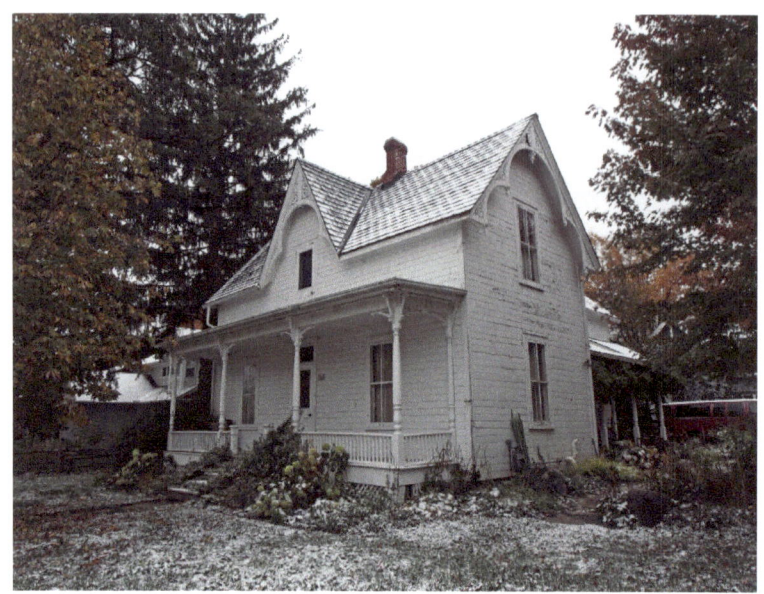
148 Brock Street East

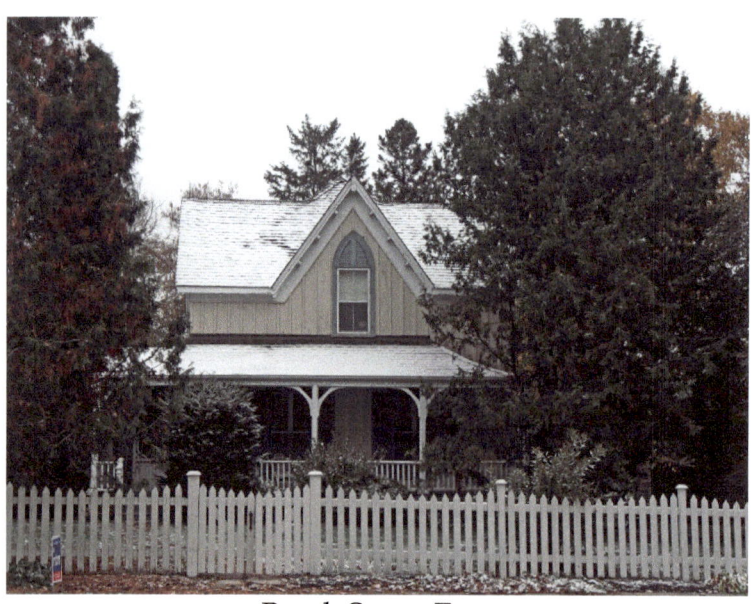
Brock Street East

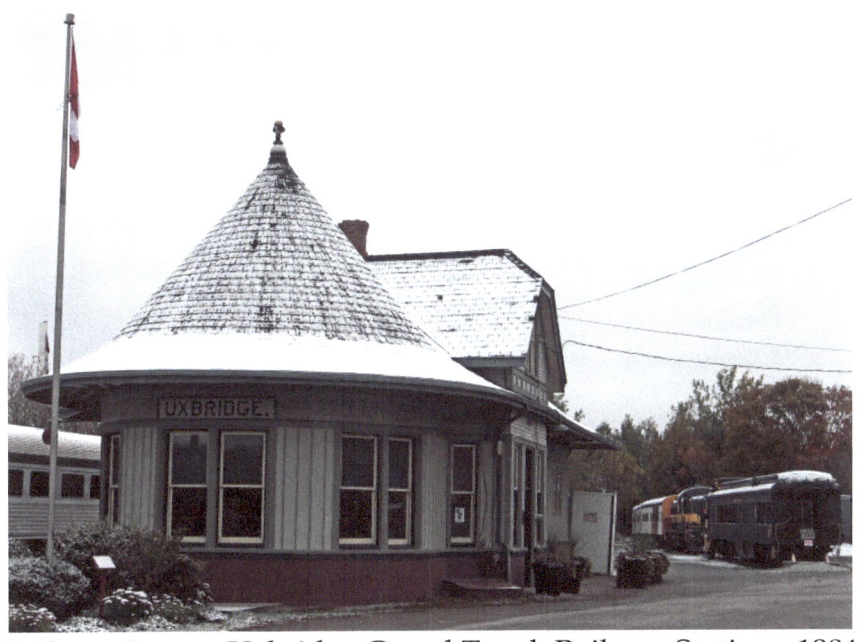

Railway Street - Uxbridge Grand Trunk Railway Station - 1904 Erected to replace an earlier station, this is an excellent example of the "witch's hat roof" style, a unique Victorian design. The foundation wall of the building is brick and the rest of the building is board and batten with clapboard on an upper wall. The interior has wainscoting and elaborate woodwork and an example of the original wall stenciling still exists. The interior and exterior were restored as closely as possible to the original. A railway museum is now housed in the baggage room.

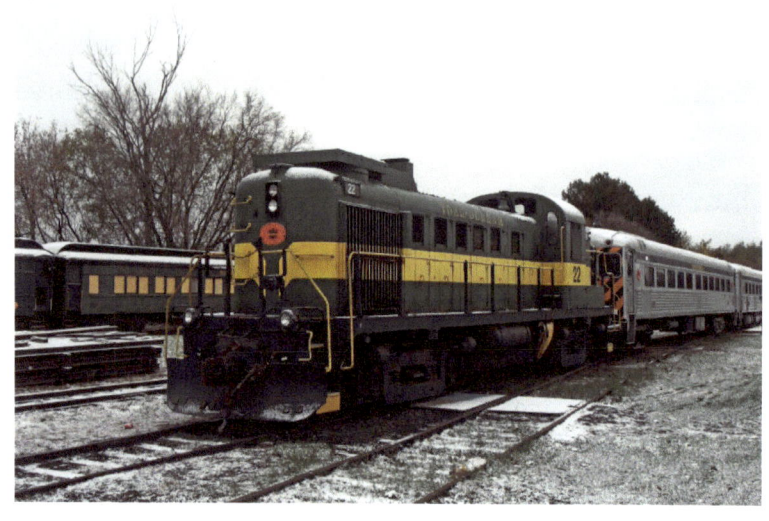

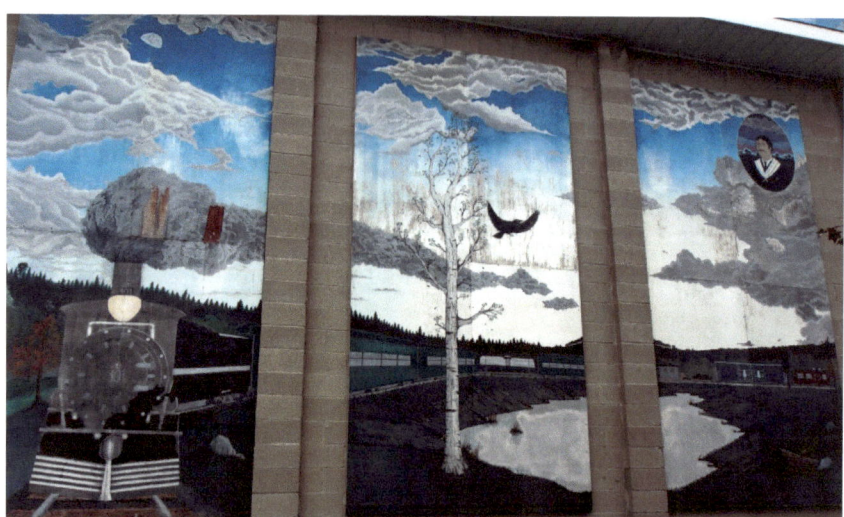

Mural

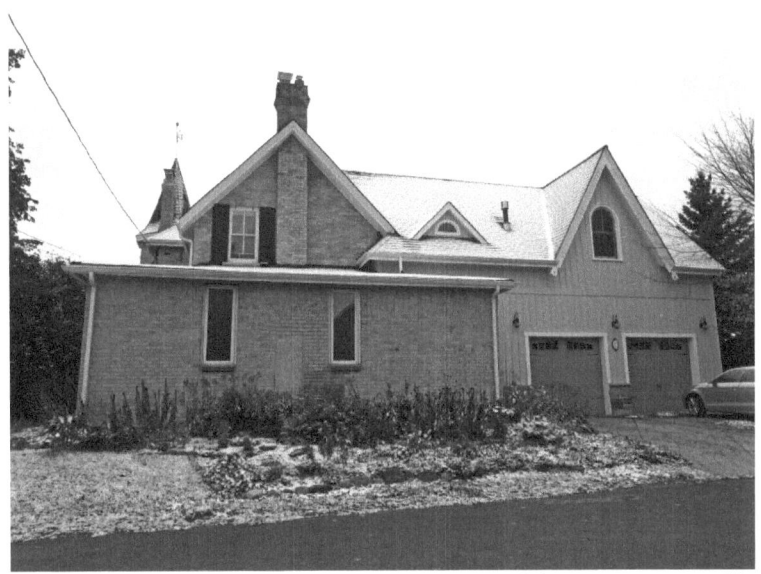

13 Young Street - Charles and Annie Gould two story yellow brick House is in Queen Anne Revival style with a steep hip roof, tall chimneys and turret. Originally owned by Joseph Gould, property was inherited by his son in 1886. Charles and brother Harvey operated Gould Brothers Bank on Brock Street and Uxbridge Roller Mills and Gould Flour & Feed Store.

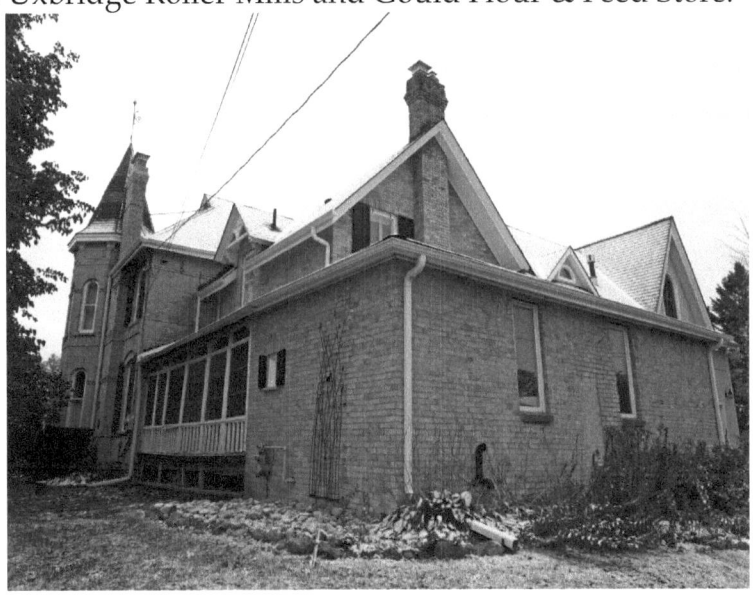

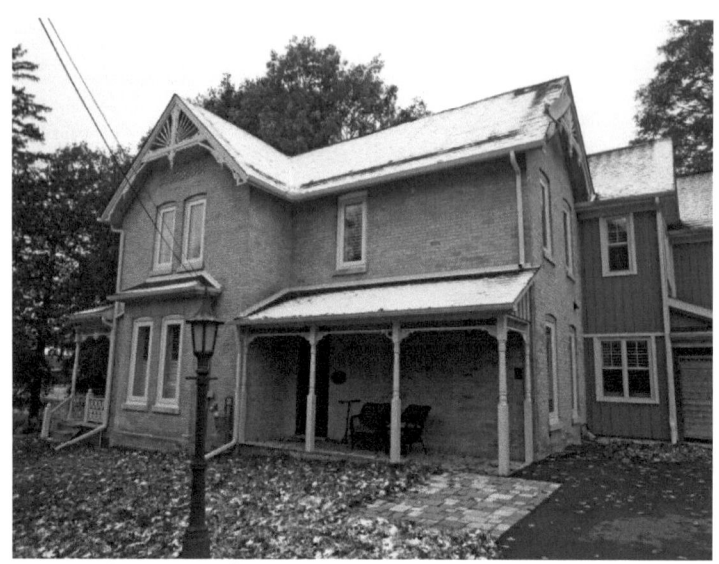

7 Dominion Street – The Patterson House is a 1½ story yellow brick home. The west peak of the gables has decorative brickwork, and intricate bargeboard, Tannery Owner – The house was built in 1888 and was bought by Andrew Patterson, who was involved in the Parrish Tannery on Bascom Street. He was also Mayor in 1891.

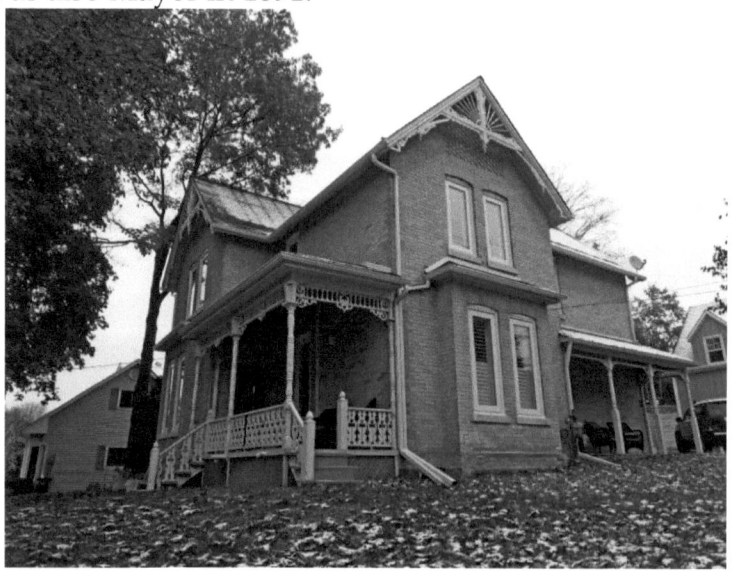

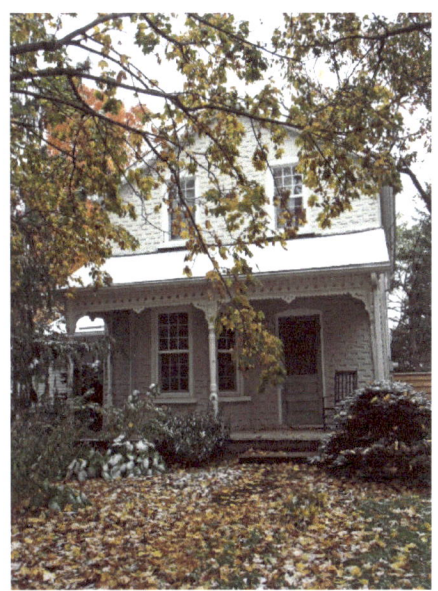

5 Dominion Street

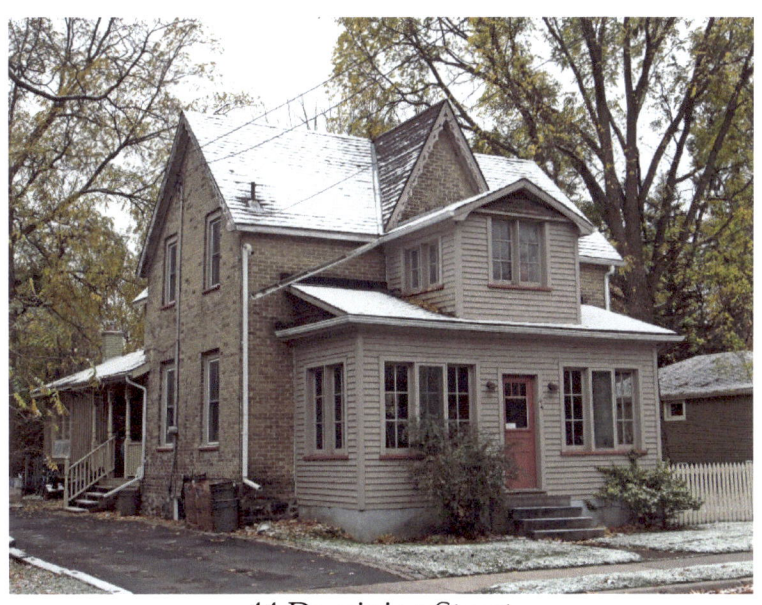

44 Dominion Street

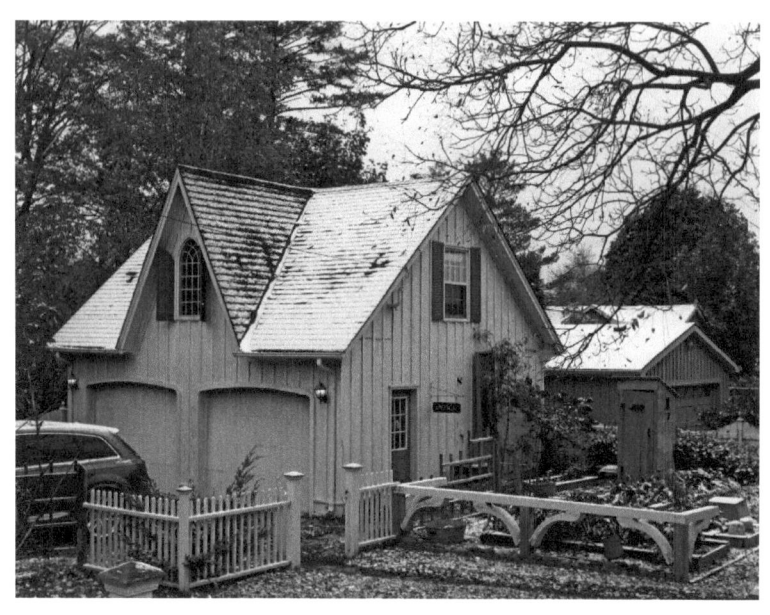

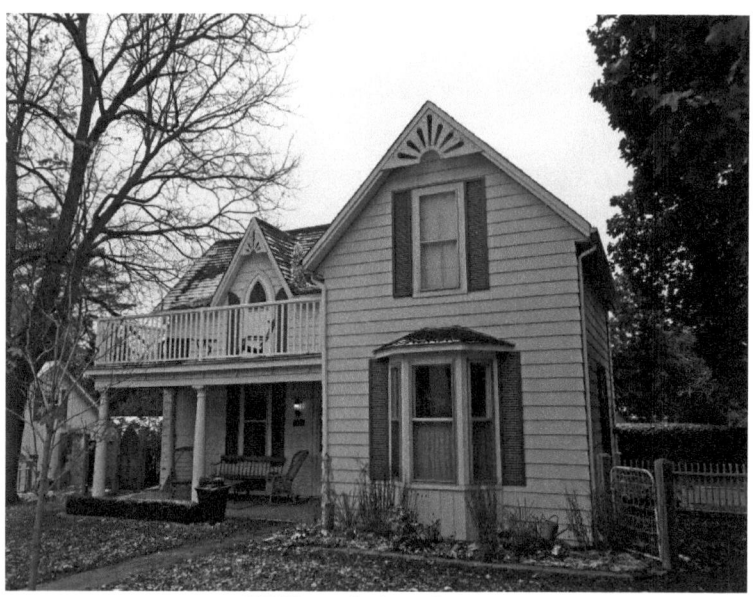

25 Dominion Street

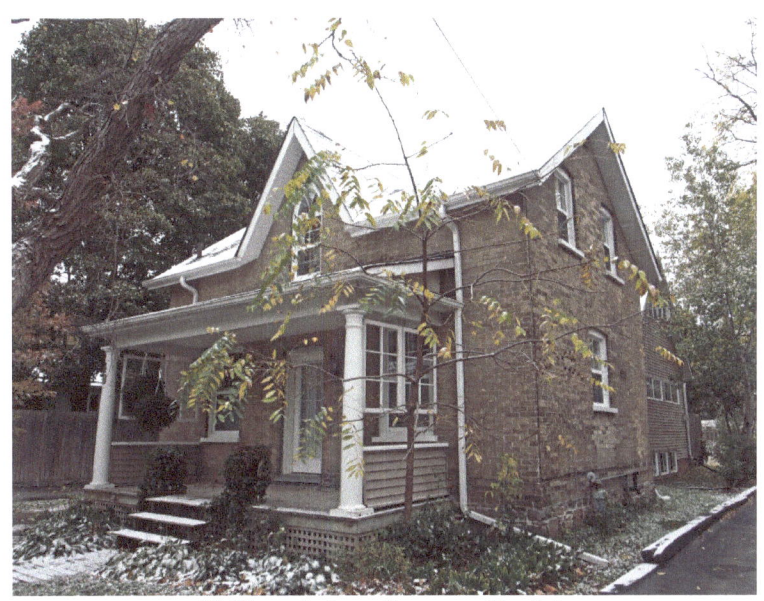

48 Dominion Street - Gothic

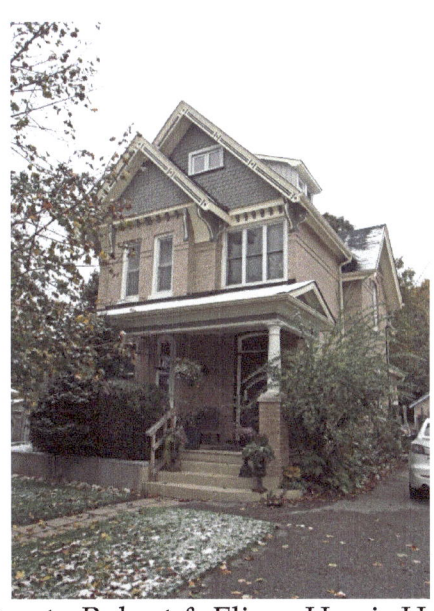

49 Dominion Street - Robert & Elinor Harris House, Lawyer & Mayor (1939-1989) – c. 1884

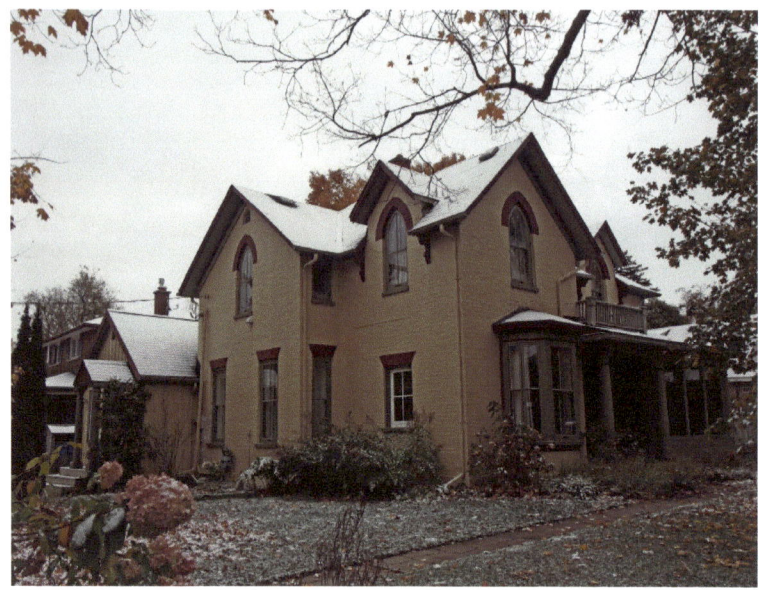

Dominion Street – bay window

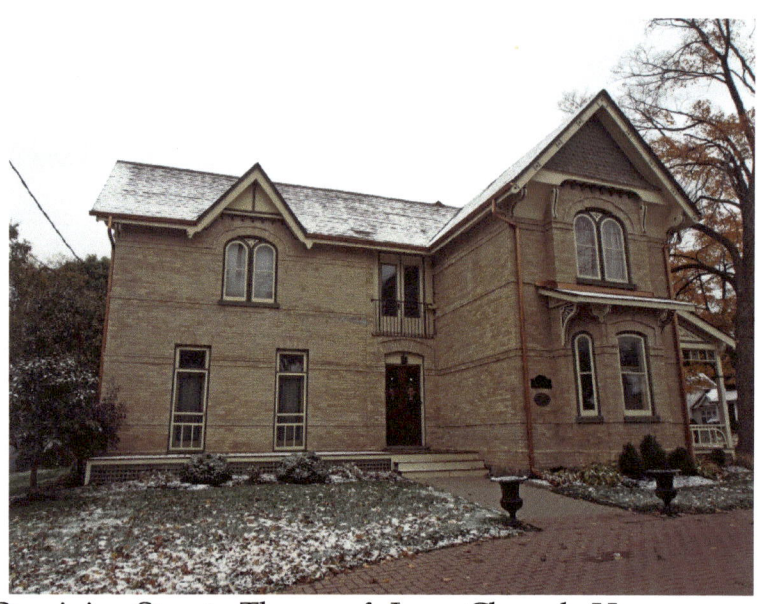

55 Dominion Street - Thomas & Lucy Chapple House, Barrister & MPP – c. 1885

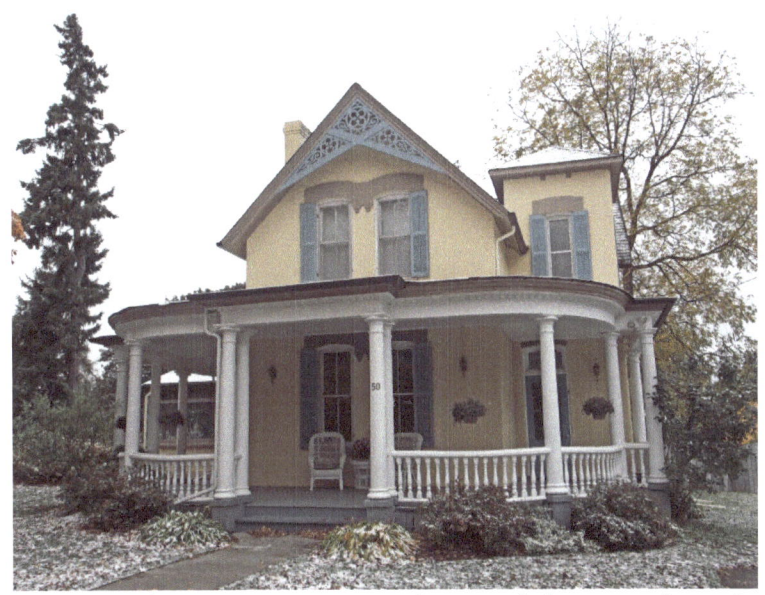

50 Dominion Street – wraparound verandah, verge board trim on gable, two-story tower

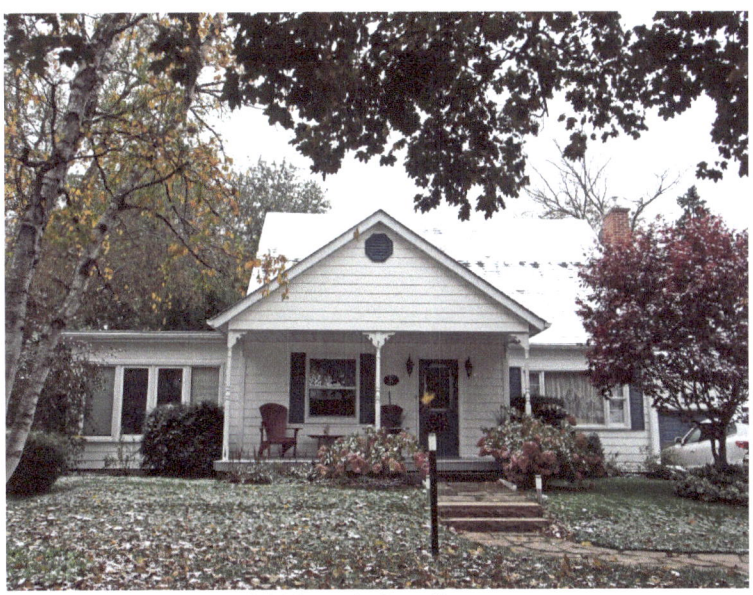

80 Dominion Street

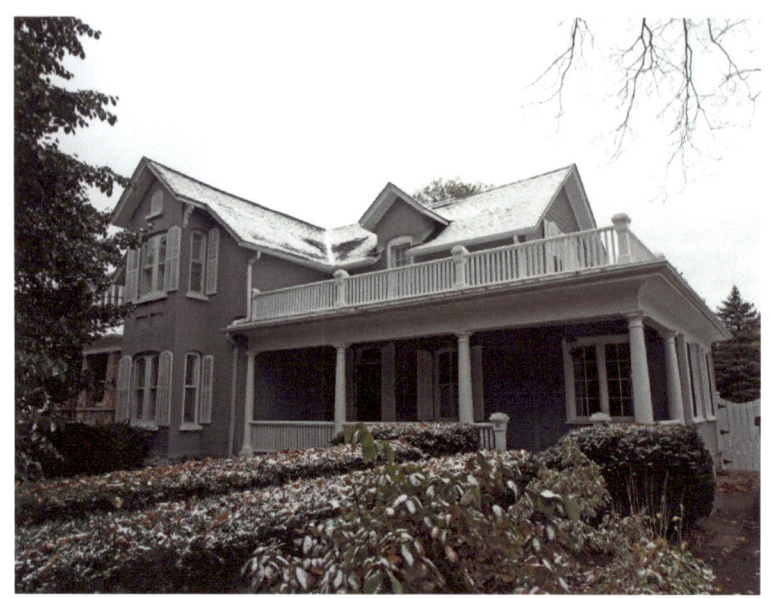
19 First Avenue

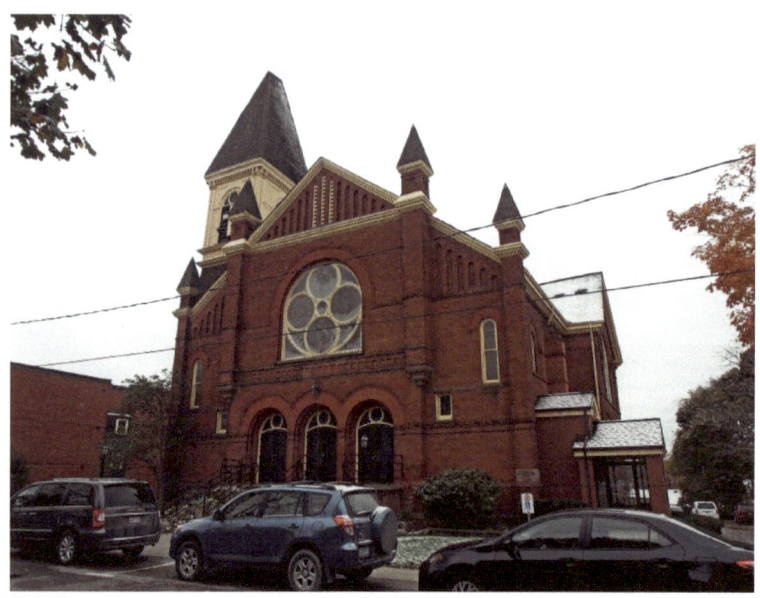
20 First Avenue – Trinity United Church – rose window

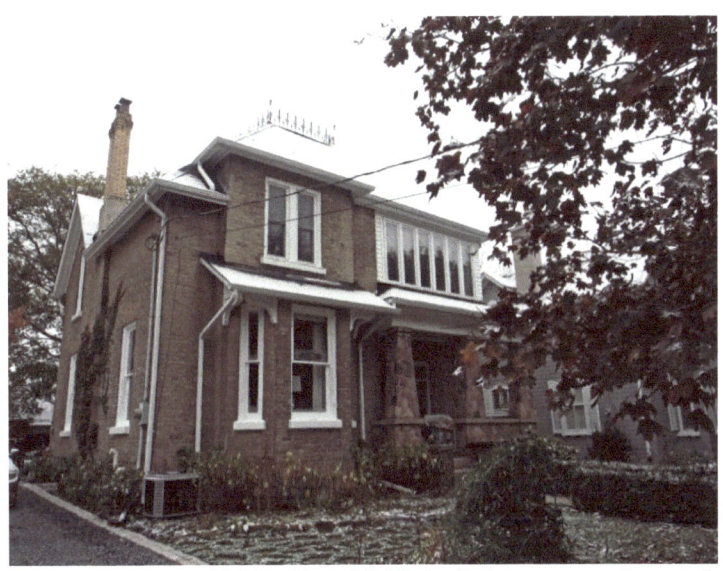

23 First Avenue - c. 1888 - David Thirsk (carpenter) purchased the lot in 1887 and built this Gothic Revival two-story yellow bricked home with a coursed fieldstone basement. In 1908 it was purchased by W.H. Brownscombe who was in the Boot and Shoe business. There is a widow's walk with iron cresting on the rooftop.

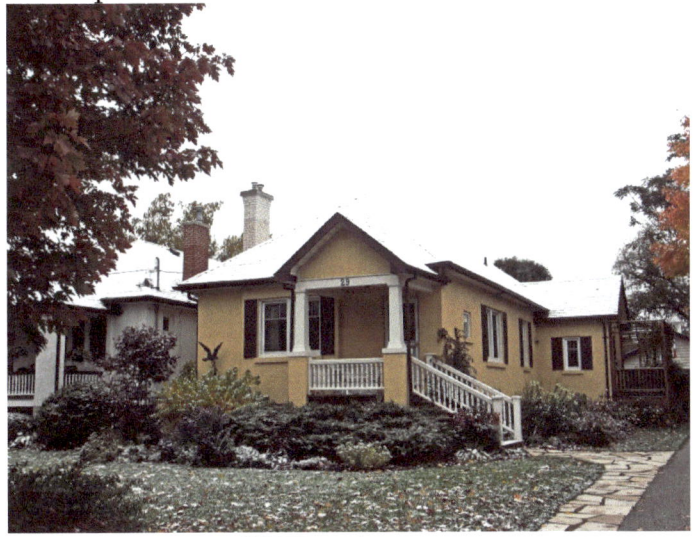

29 First Avenue

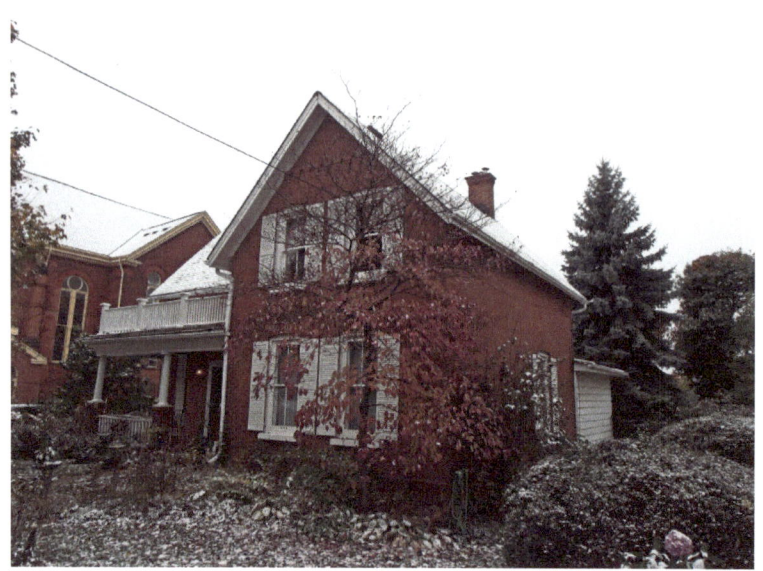

First Avenue

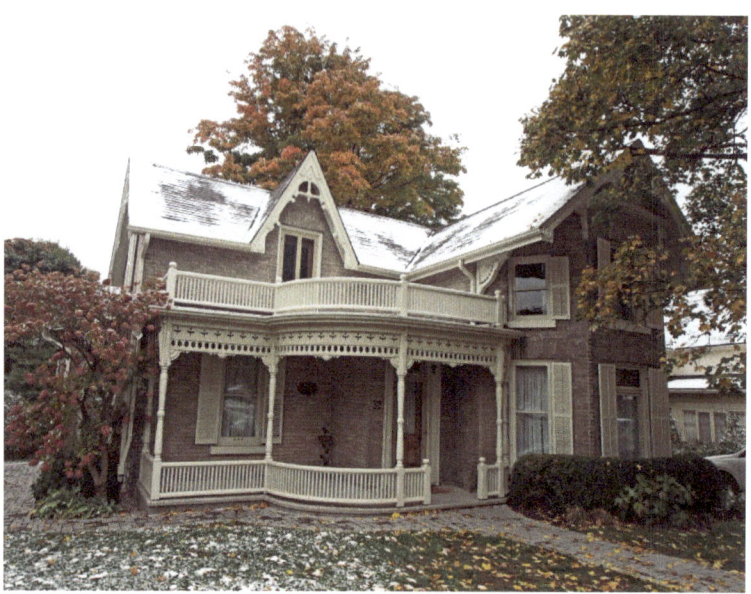

32 First Avenue - Samuel & Emma Todd House, Carriage Builder (1885-1906) – c. 1884 – Gothic Revival – verge board trim on gables

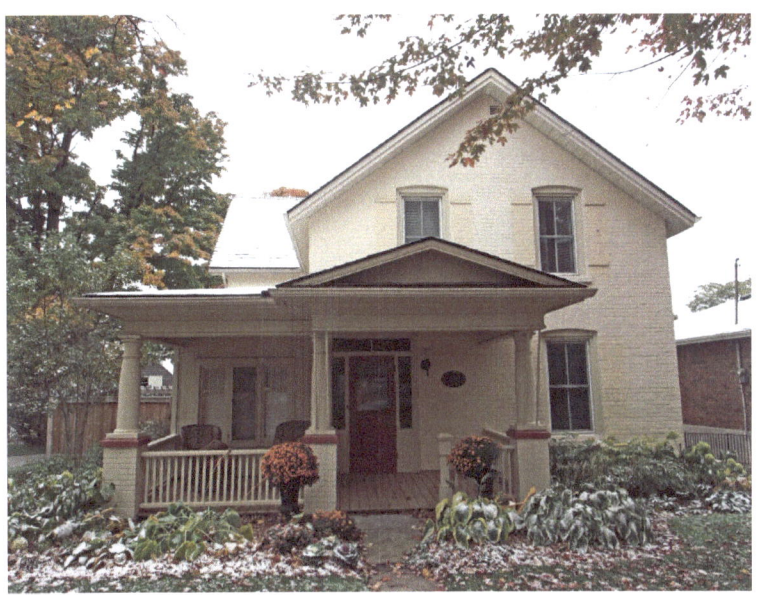

First Avenue – Silas Beebe House, Blacksmith – c. 1875

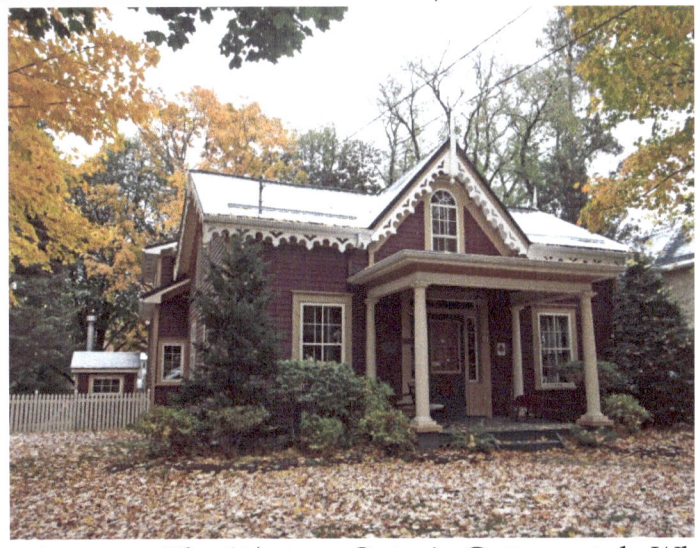

41 First Avenue - The 1½ story Ontario Cottage style Wheler House was built in 1860 by Edward Wheler at the northwest corner of Brock and Main Street with the lumber coming from the local mill owned by George Wheler. It was moved to its present location by Ira G. Crosby in 1871. He was the Town Treasurer for many years.

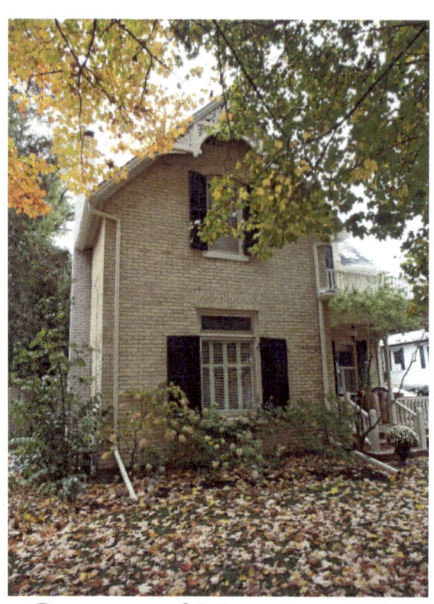

37 First Avenue - George and Mary Long House built in 1885 by George Long a local builder and mason. The house is a Victorian Gothic 1½ story yellow brick home with ornate bargeboard on all the gables and verandah. There is a small upper and lower verandah off to the side and the front and the upper verandah has a door and railing around.

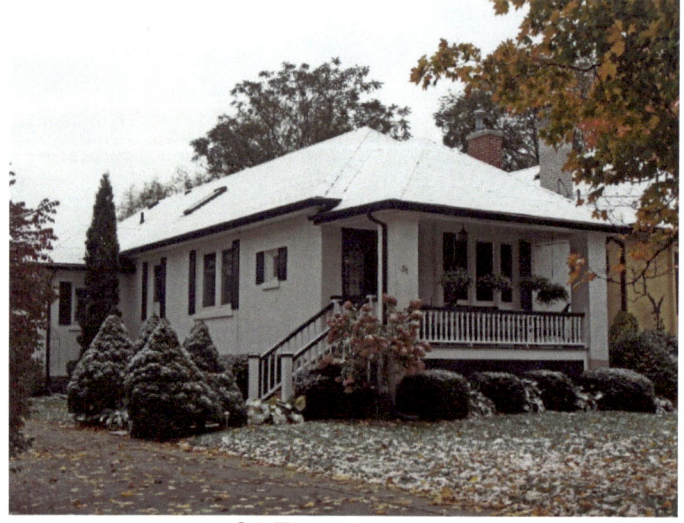

31 First Avenue

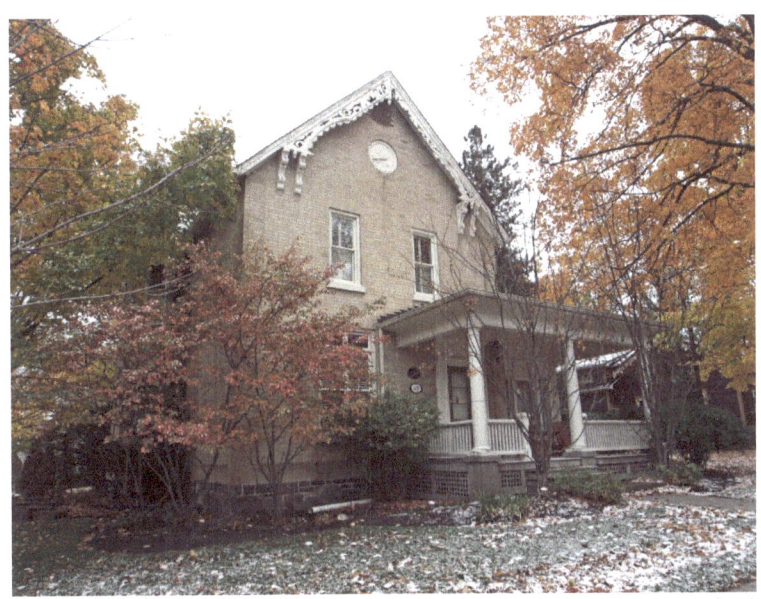

49 First Avenue - The 1½ story Ontario Cottage style Wheler House was built in 1860 by Edward Wheler (miller) at the northwest corner of Brock and Main Street with the lumber coming from the local mill owned by George Wheler. It was moved to its present location by Ira G. Crosby (Town Treasurer) in 1871.

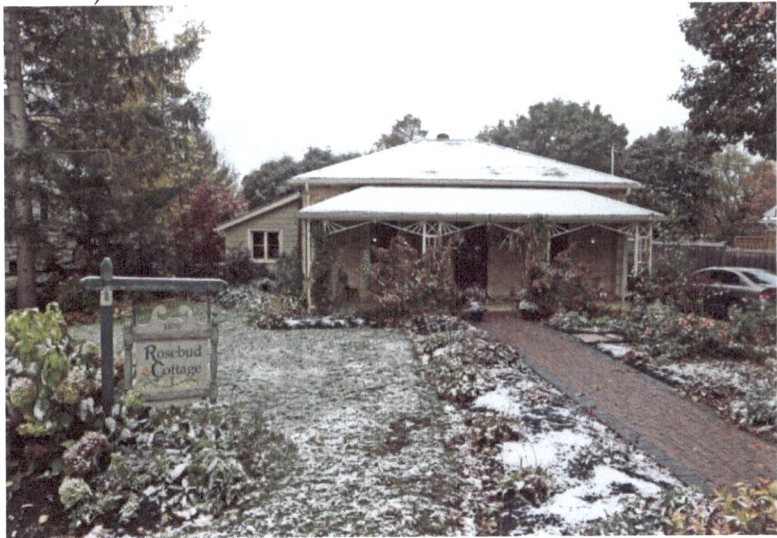

72 First Avenue – Ontario Cottage

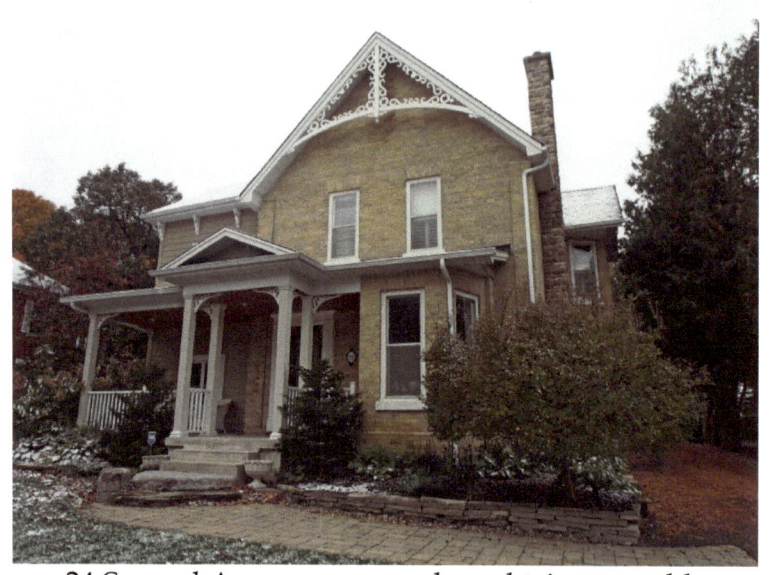
24 Second Avenue – verge board trim on gable

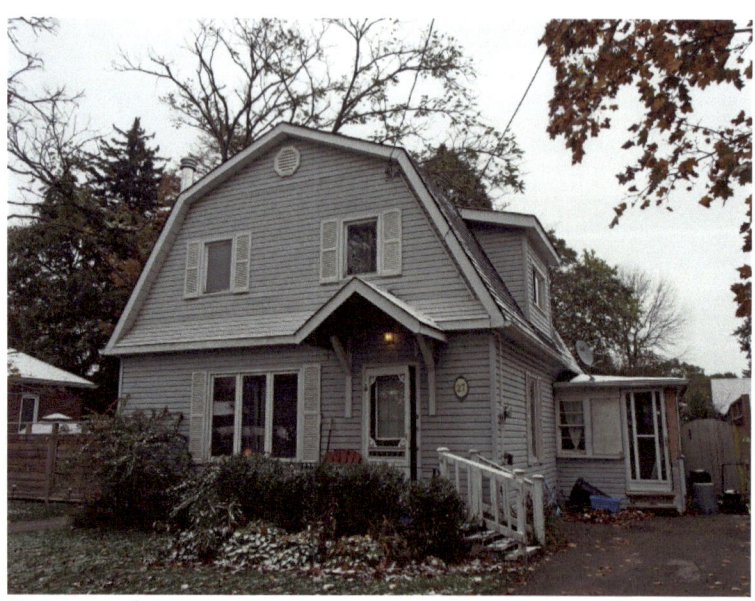
27 Second Avenue – Neo-Colonial style – gambrel roof

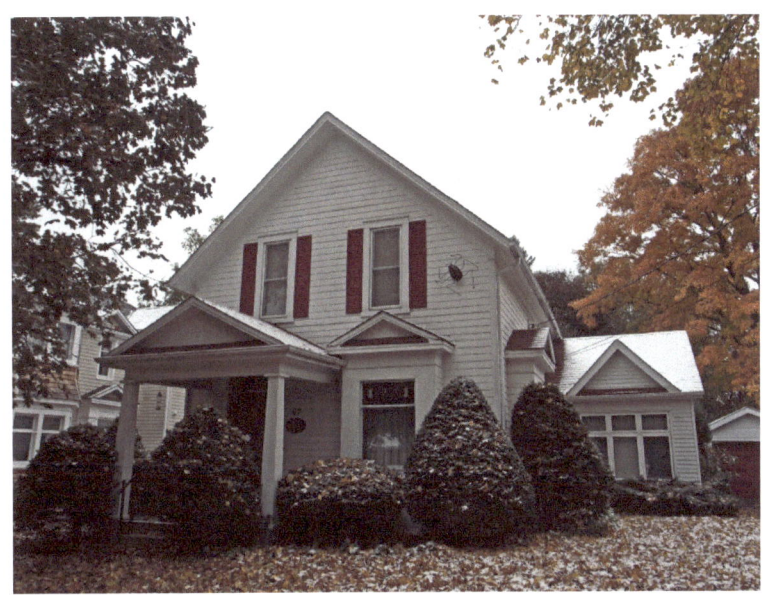

67 Second Avenue - Thomas & Alma Gould House, Furrier (1888-1961) – c. 1877

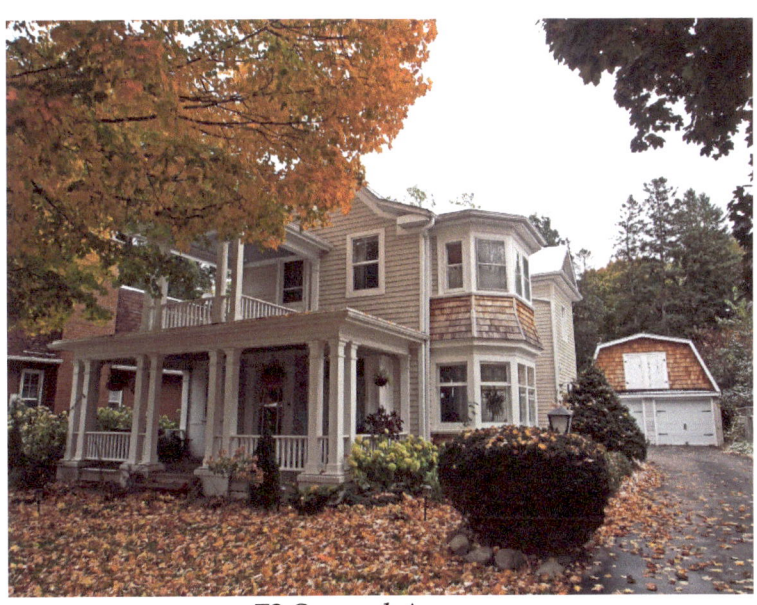

73 Second Avenue

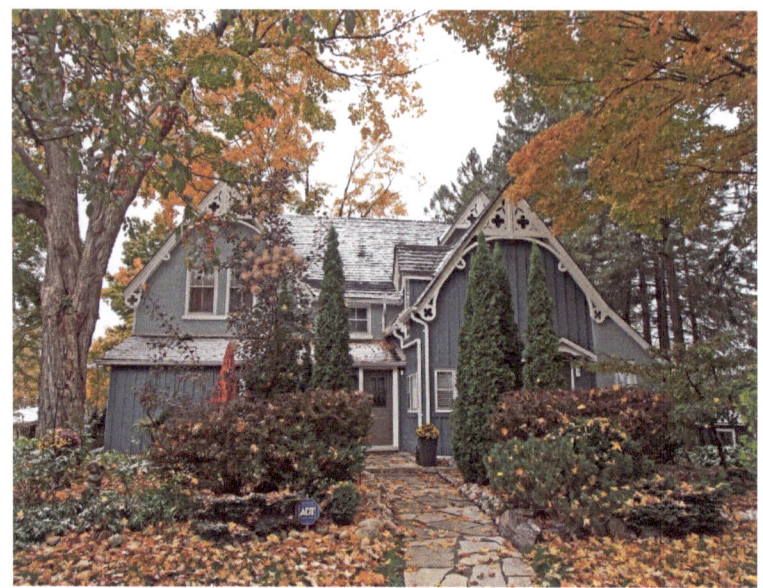

84 Second Avenue - Joseph E. & Elizabeth Gould House, Farmer – c. 1875

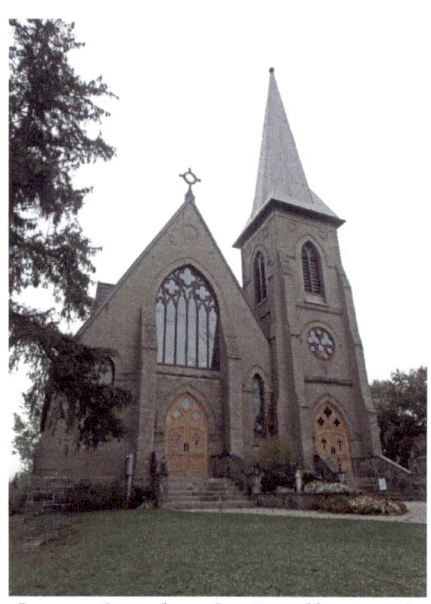

59 Toronto Street South – St. Paul's Anglican Church

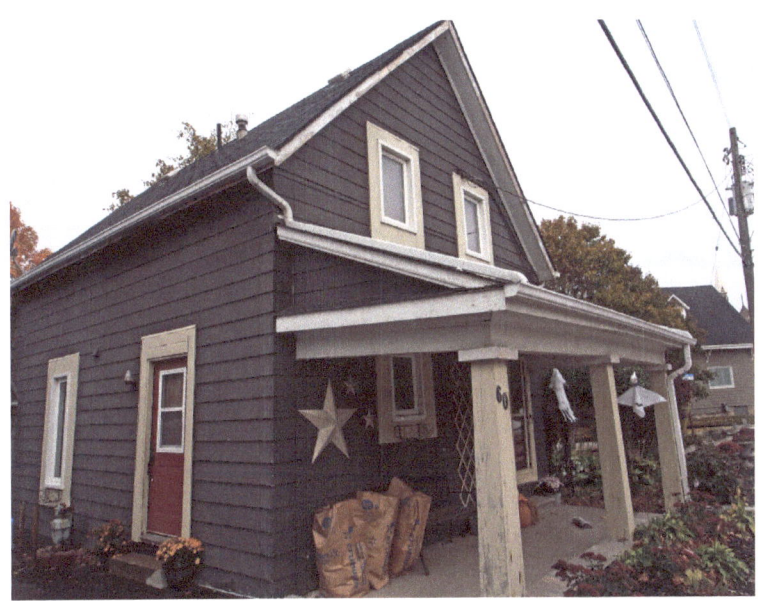

60 Toronto Street South

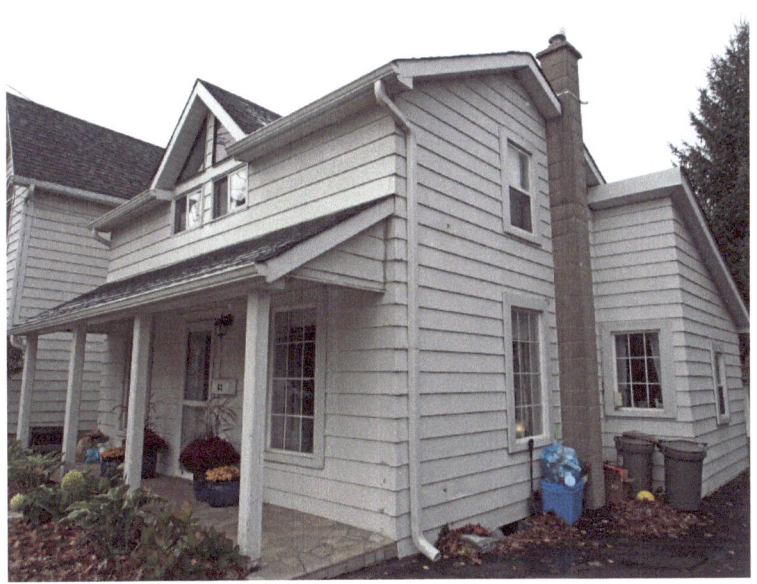

62 Toronto Street South

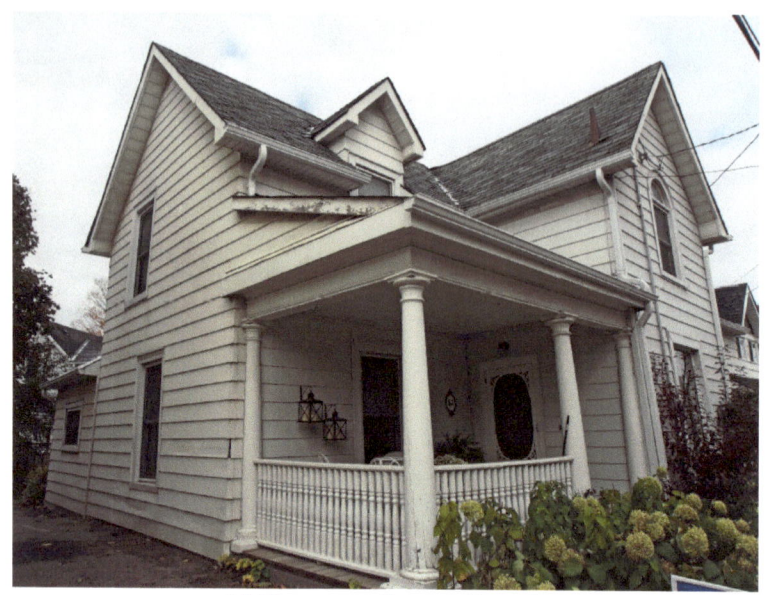
64 Toronto Street South

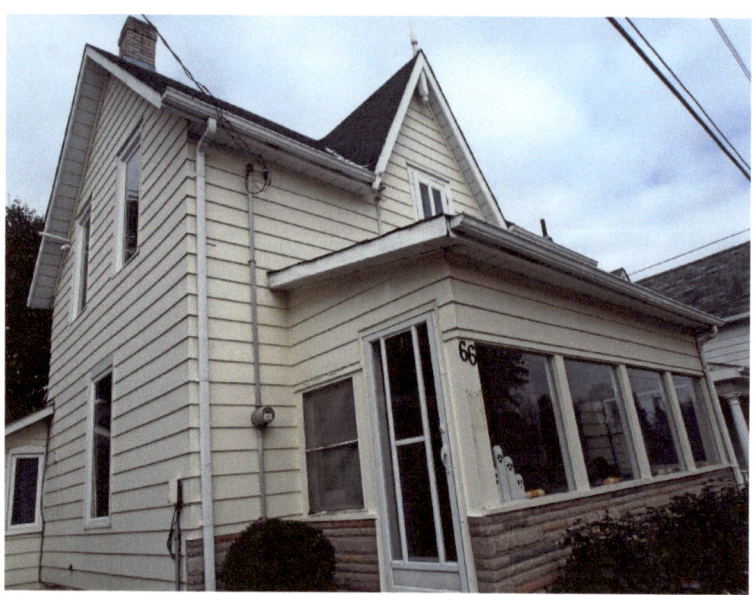
66 Toronto Street South

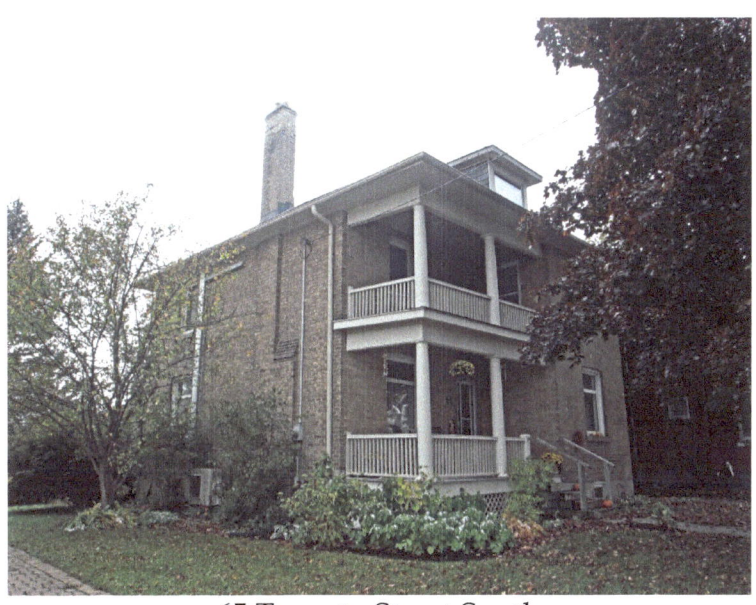

65 Toronto Street South

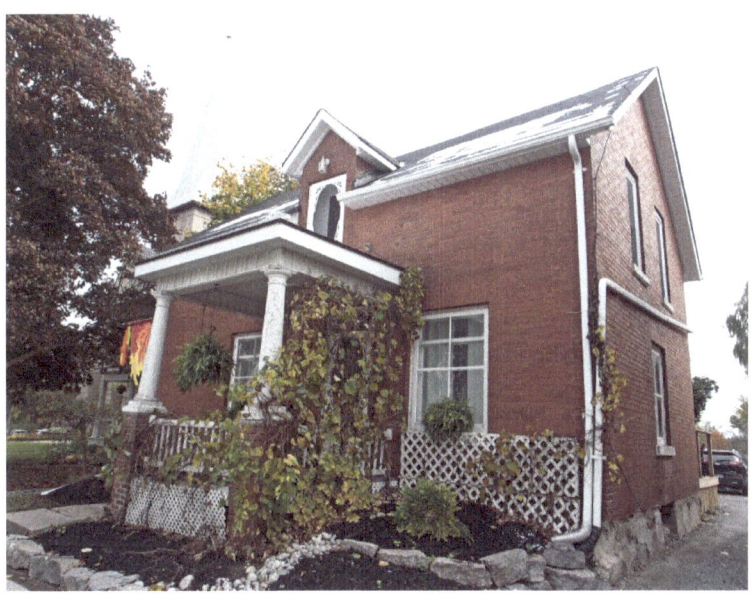

67 Toronto Street South

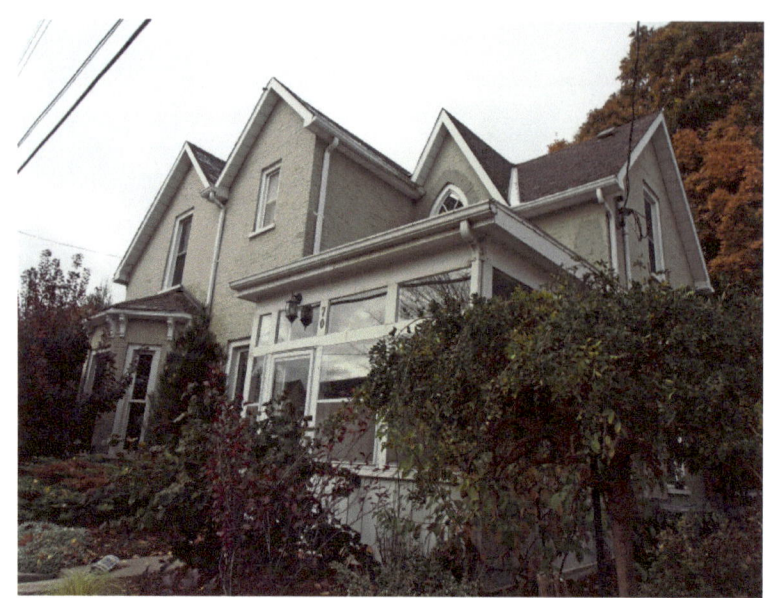

70 Toronto Street South

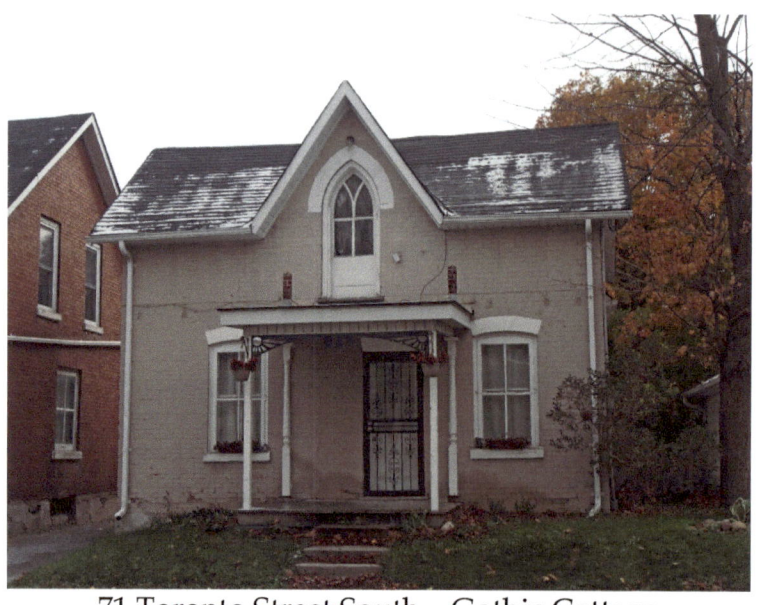

71 Toronto Street South – Gothic Cottage

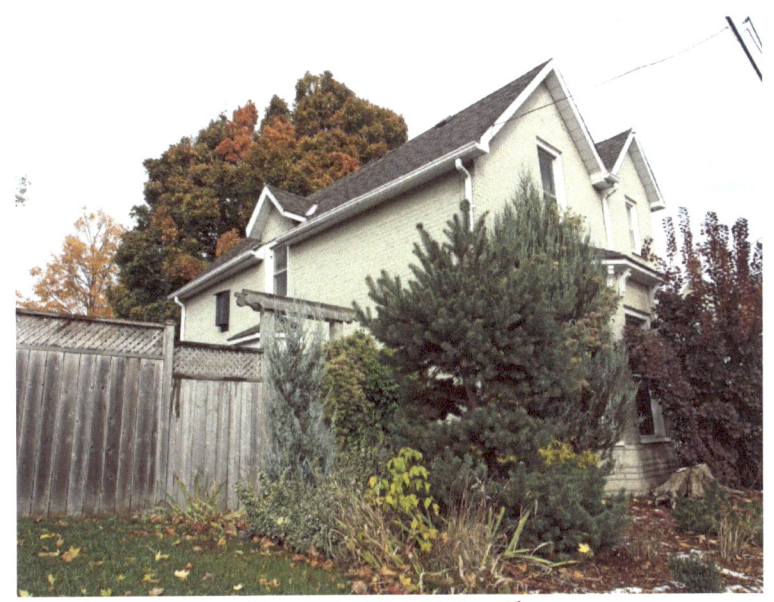

Toronto Street South

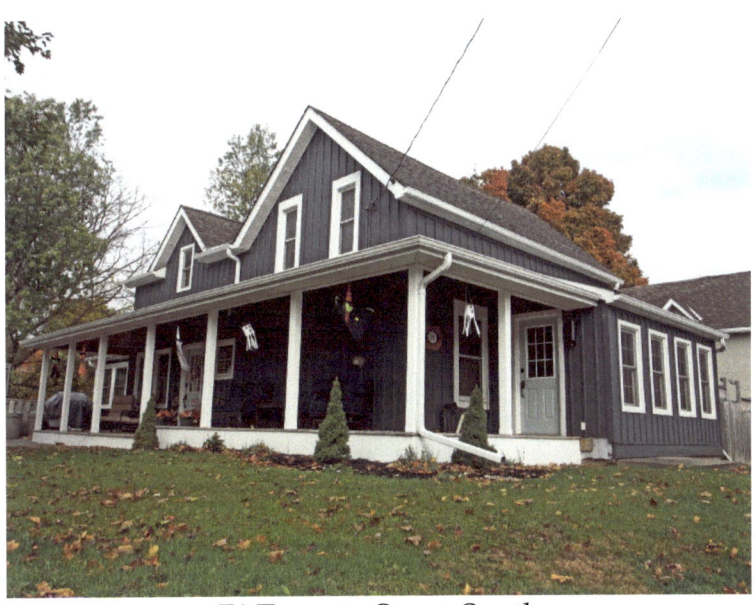

74 Toronto Street South

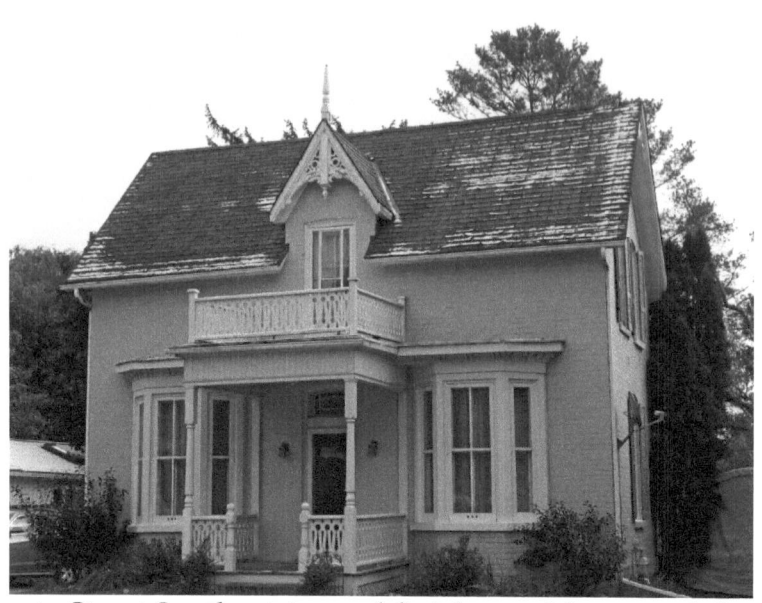

Toronto Street South – trim and finial on gable, second-floor balcony

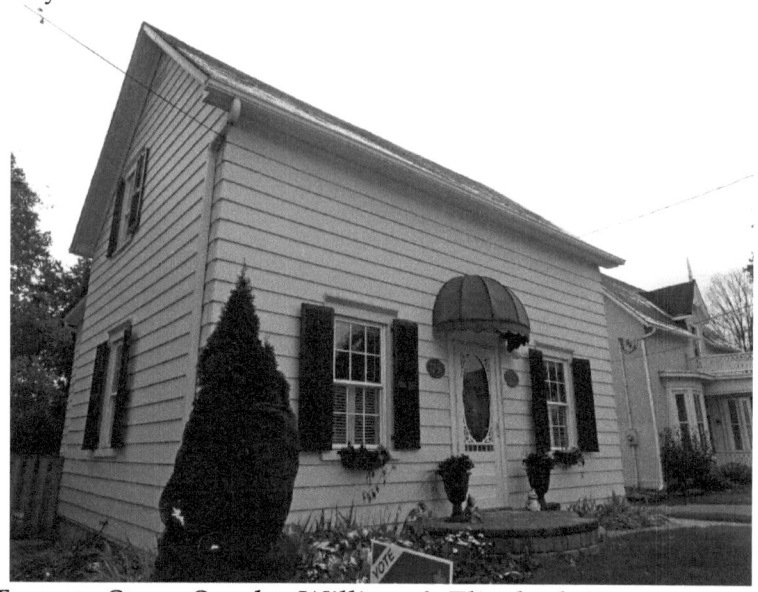

75 Toronto Street South - William & Elizabeth Ferguson House, Retired Gentleman Farmer - c 1872

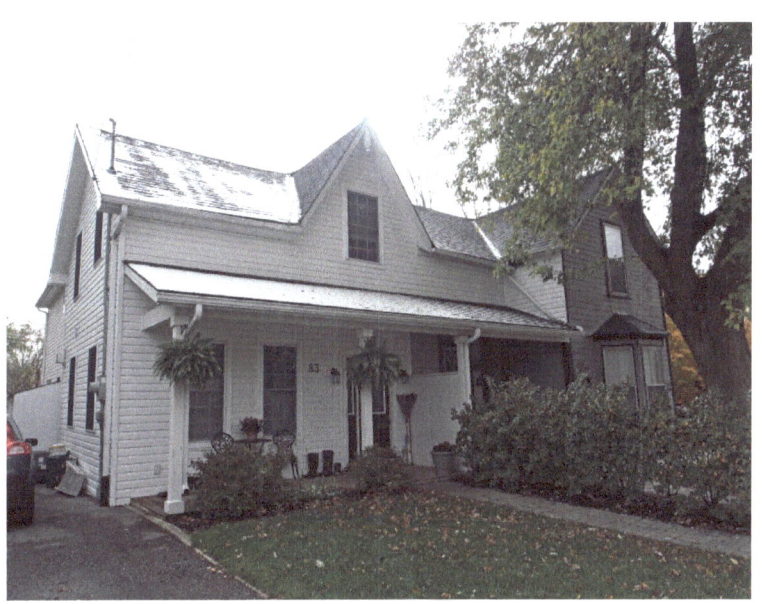

83 Toronto Street South

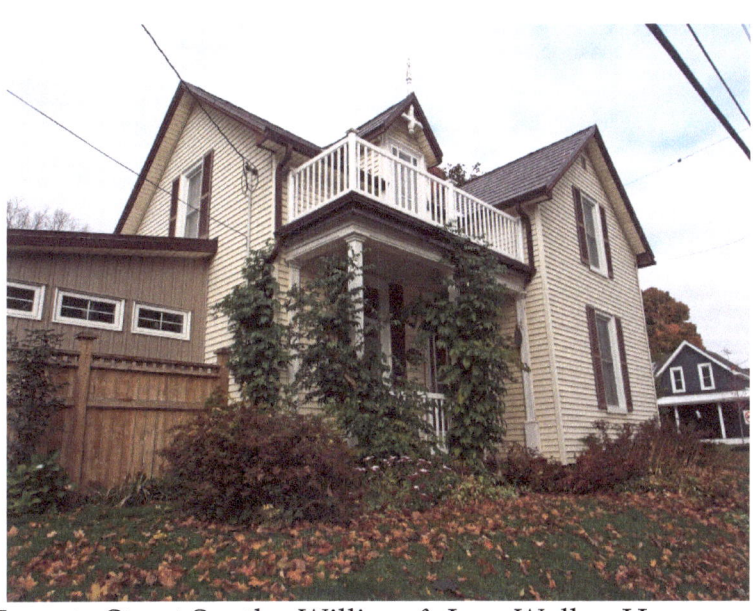

84 Toronto Street South - William & Jane Walker House, Carpenter/Builder – c. 1878

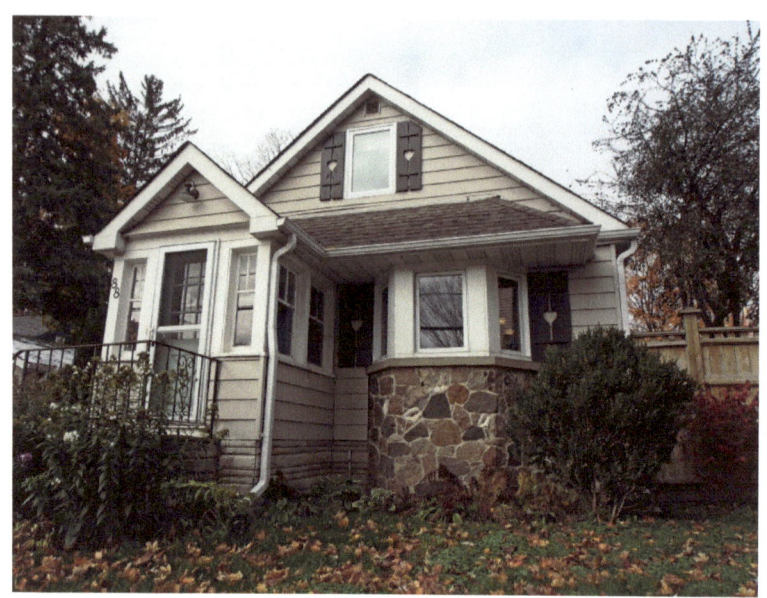

88 Toronto Street South

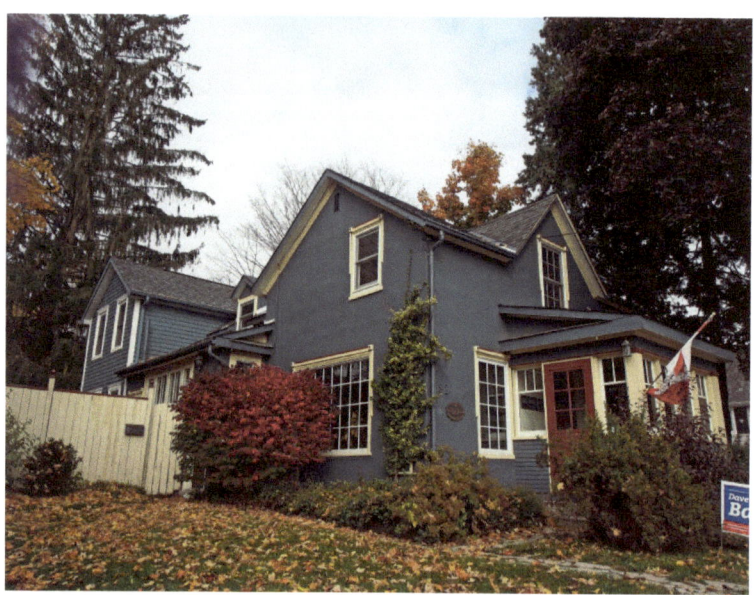

92 Toronto Street South - Samuel & Jane McKinnell House, Merchant – c. 1871

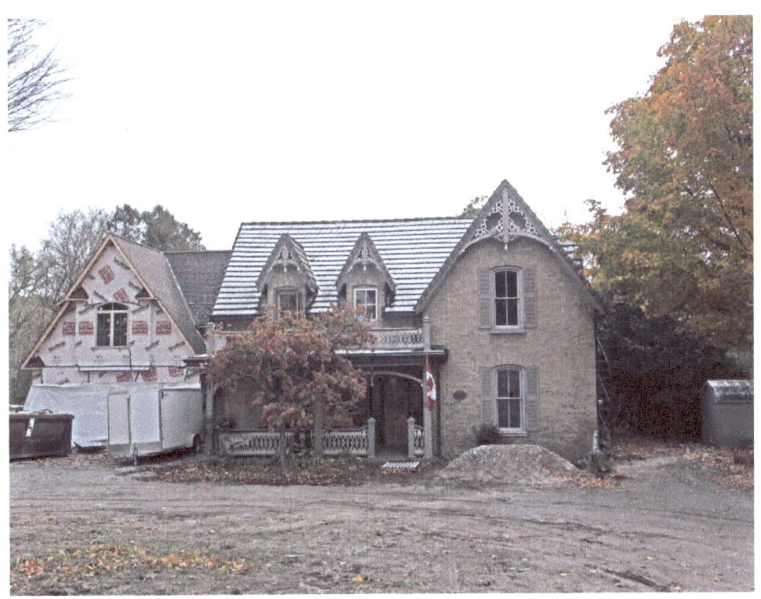

89 Toronto Street South - Presbyterian Church Manse (1881-1981) – c. 1875 – It is a large L-shaped 1½ story home of white brick. Gables have barge board. Door on second floor opens to a railed verandah. Windows are rounded on top and casements appear to be dated from the 1870s. Foundation is dressed fieldstone.

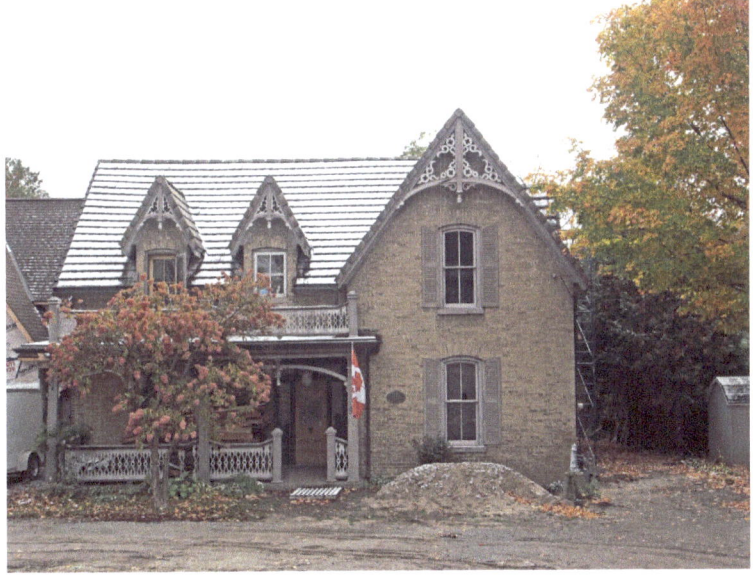

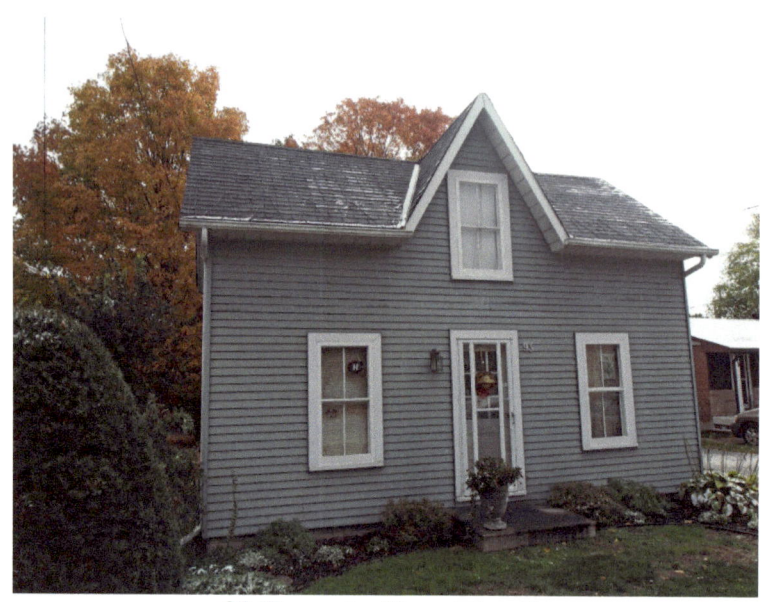

93 Toronto Street South

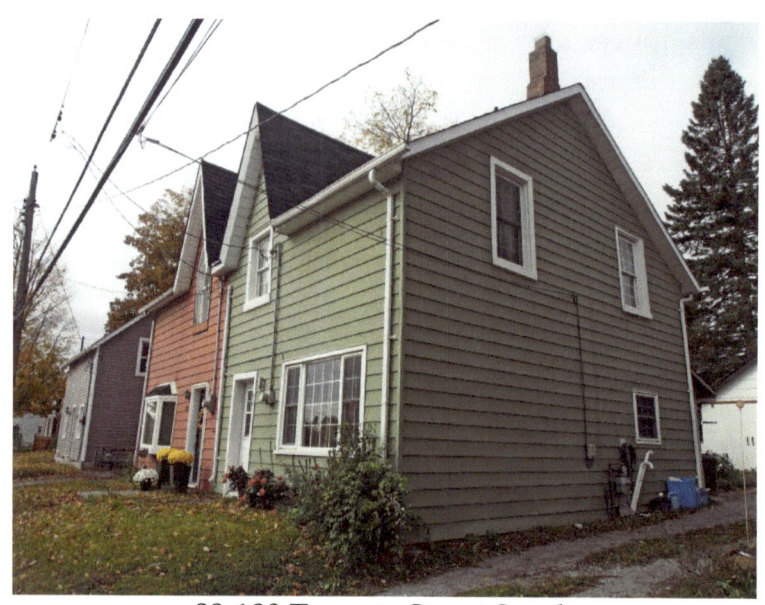

98-100 Toronto Street South

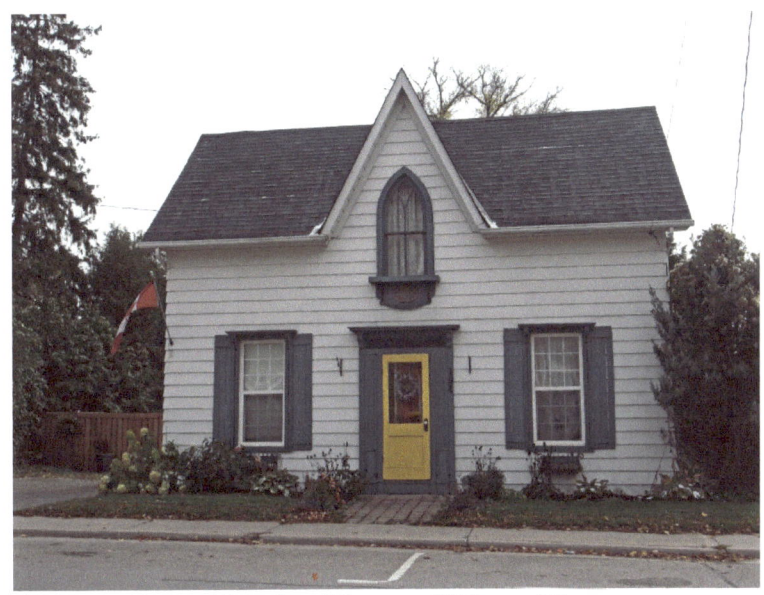

101 Toronto Street South - Warren Wilson House, Wheelwright – c. 1858

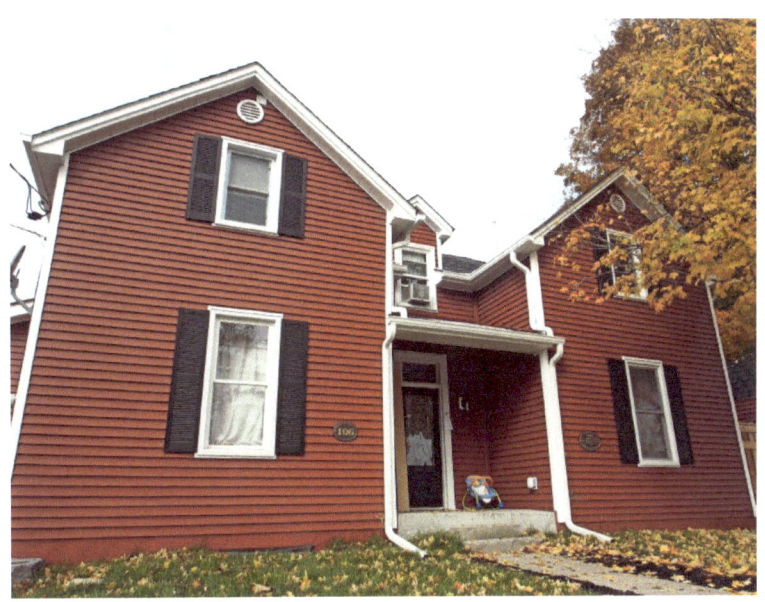

106 Toronto Street South - Alexander & Catharine Thompson House, Carpenter & Hotel Owner – c. 1865

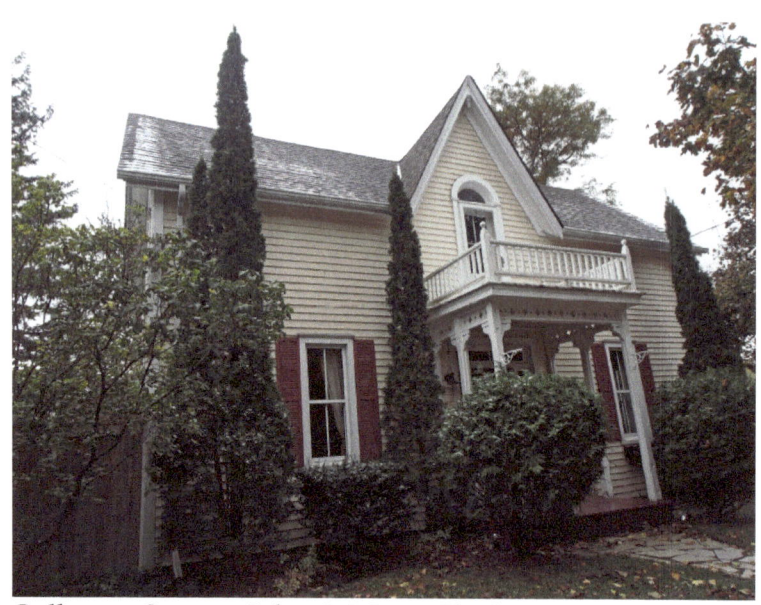

112 Colborne Street - John & Mary Clark House, Grain Dealer – c. 1875

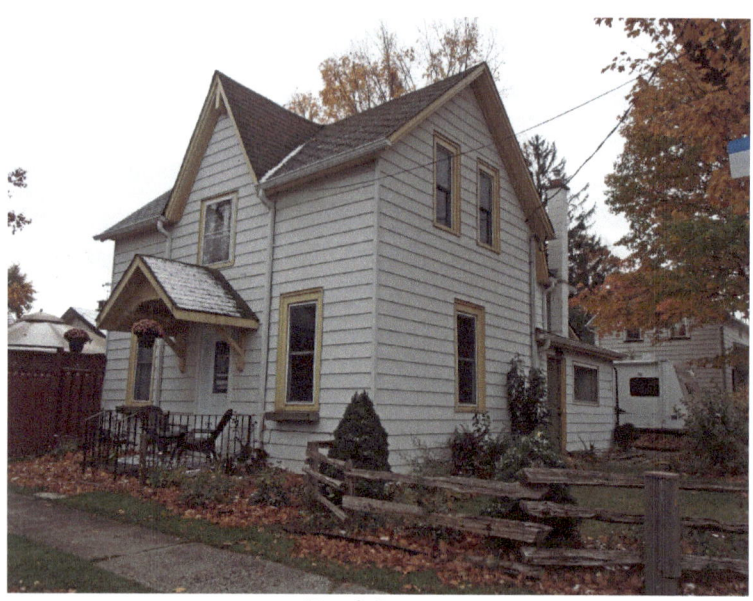

Peel Street

An Uxbridge Story in Stone by Artist Fly Freeman

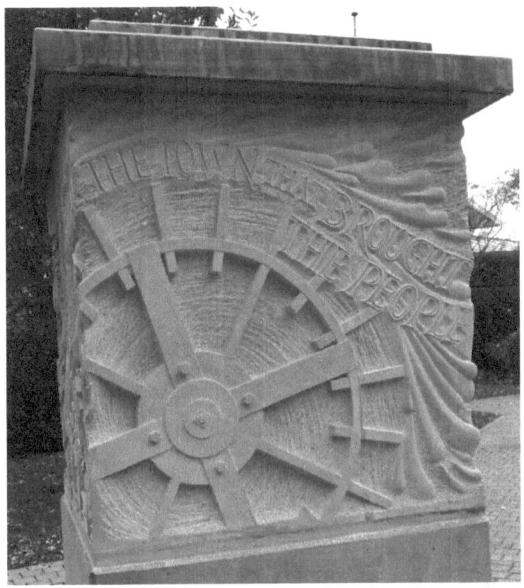

The Town That Brought the People

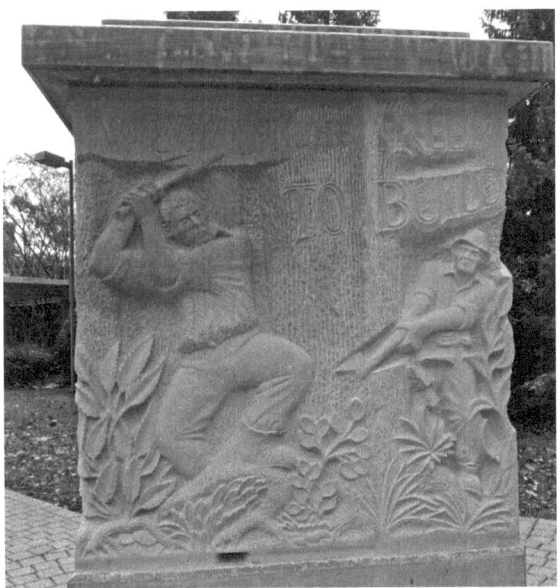

We Cut the Trees to Build

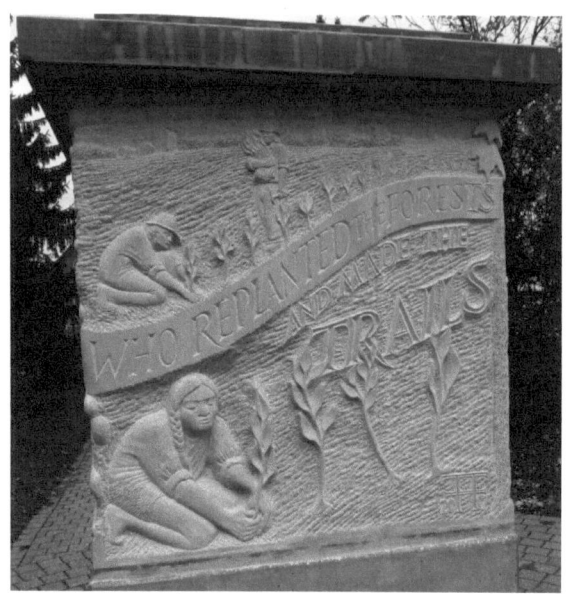

Who Planted Forests

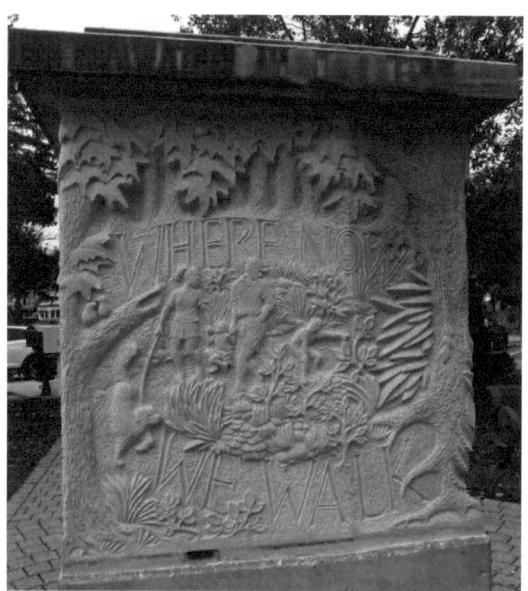

Where Now We Walk

Building Styles

Gothic Revival, 1830-1890 – These decorative buildings have sharply-pitched gables with highly detailed verge boards, pointed-arch window openings, and dichromatic brickwork. It is a common style in Ontario.

Italianate, 1850-1900 – A two story rectangular building with a mild hip roof, a projecting frontispiece, and generous eaves with ornate cornice brackets was the basis of the style; often there are large sash windows, quoins, ornate detailing on the windows, belvederes and wraparound verandahs. Italianate commercial buildings often have cast iron cresting and elegant window surrounds.

Neo-Colonial (also Colonial Revival, Georgian Revival or Neo-Georgian) architecture seeks to revive elements of architectural style of American colonial architecture of the period around the Revolutionary War which drew strongly from Georgian architecture of Great Britain. Architecture from the 18th and early 19th centuries in Ontario includes a wide assortment of detailing and ornament applied to a design centered around the fireplace and the source of water. Structures are typically two stories, have a symmetrical front facade with elaborate front doorways, often with decorative crown pediments, fanlights, and sidelights, symmetrical windows flanking the front entrance, often in pairs or threes, and columned porches.

Ontario Cottage - one or one-and-a-half story buildings with a cottage or hip roof. The cottage roof is an equal hip roof where each hip extends to a point in the center of the roof. The hip roof has a long hip in the center. The Ontario Cottage is the vernacular design of the Regency Cottage which generally has a more ornate doorway and a partial or full verandah surrounding it. The roof can have a dormer, a belvedere, and generally two chimneys.

Queen Anne, 1885-1900 – This style is distinguished by an irregular outline featuring a combination of an offset tower, broad gables, projecting two-story bays, verandahs, multi-sloped roofs, and tall, decorative chimneys. A mixture of brick and wood is common. Windows often have one large single-paned bottom sash and small panes in the upper sash.

Victorian - In Ontario, a Victorian style building can be seen as any building built between 1840 and 1900 that doesn't fit into any of the other categories. It encompasses a large group of buildings constructed in brick, stone, and timber, using an eclectic mixture of Classical and Gothic motifs.

Other Books by Barbara Raue

Coins of Gold
Arrows, Indians and Love
The Life and Times of Barbara
The Cromwell Family Book
Laura Secord Discovered
Daddy Where Are You?

Montana Series
Book 1: Montana Dream
Book 2: Life on the Montana Frontier
Book 3: Montana to Boston and Back
Book 4: Montana Sons Go to War
Book 5: Montana Sons Return from War

Donaldson Series
Book 1: Rite of Passage
Book 2: Rite of Marriage

© 2022 by Barbara Raue - All the photos in this book have been taken with my cameras. I own the rights to them.

Barbara is The Authority on Saving Our History One Photo at a Time. She is pursuing her interest in photography and architecture by preserving a record through photos of old buildings from the 1800s and 1900s with their unique architecture. Enjoy the beautiful architecture in the comfort of your living room. Dream about what it was like in those by-gone days. Dream about what it was like to live in a mansion like one of those in this book.

Barbara Raue, a wife, mother and grandmother, is an avid reader and writer. She has researched and compiled several family histories. In 2010, Barbara published her book "Coins of Gold," which celebrates the courageous life of her mother, May Todd. Barbara's second book is a historical fiction "Arrows, Indians and Love" which takes place in Boonesborough, Kentucky during the time of Daniel Boone. In 2013, Barbara published *The Cromwell Family Book* in which she traces her ancestry generations back into Great Britain. Her second novel is called *Laura Secord Discovered,* in which the story of Laura's service during the War of 1812 is shared. Barbara's memoir is titled *Daddy Where Are You?* It tells of her life growing up without a father. Five novels in the Montana Series have been published, *Montana Dream, Life on the Montana Frontier, Montana to Boston and Back, Montana Sons Go to War,* and *Montana Sons Return from War.* The Donaldson series of two novels is available: *Rite of Passage* and *Rite of Marriage.*

This is a link to Barbara's website to view all of her books
http://barbararaue.ca

www.ingramcontent.com/pod-product-compliance
Lightning Source LLC
Chambersburg PA
CBHW040228220526
45473CB00001B/163